Building the Getty

Richard Meier   Building the Getty

Alfred A. Knopf / New York / 1997

This Is a Borzoi Book
Published by Alfred A. Knopf, Inc.

Copyright © 1997 by Richard Meier

All rights reserved under International
and Pan-American Copyright Conven-
tions. Published in the United States by
Alfred A. Knopf, Inc., New York, and
simultaneously in Canada by Random
House of Canada Limited, Toronto.
Distributed by Random House, Inc.,
New York.

http://www.randomhouse.com/

Owing to limitations of space,
acknowledgments for permission to
reprint previously published material
may be found on page 207.

Library of Congress Cataloging-in-
Publication Data
Meier, Richard.
Building the Getty / by Richard Meier —
1st ed.
    p.   cm.
"A Borzoi book."
Published simultaneously in Canada by
Random House of Canada Limited,
Toronto.
ISBN 0-375-40043-5 (hardcover)
1. Getty Center (Los Angeles, Calif.)
2. Art centers—California—Los Angeles.
3. Richard Meier & Partners.
4. Los Angeles (Calif.)—Buildings,
structures, etc.   I. Title.
NA6813.U62L76   1997
708.194'93—dc21   97-29326   CIP

Manufactured in the United States
of America

First Edition

For all those who dedicated themselves to making the Getty Center a reality

Acknowledgments

This book would not have been possible without the encouragement and assistance of a number of talented people.

At Knopf I am grateful to Sonny Mehta for his vision and support of the project and to Shelley Wanger for her herculean diligence as my editor. Massimo Vignelli, as always, has designed a beautiful book, which Iris Weinstein was able to skillfully execute. This book would probably not exist if it were not for the persistence of the literary agent Ed Victor, who encouraged me to pursue this endeavor. In my Los Angeles office, Lori East provided dedicated assistance in transcribing and resurrecting notes. In New York, indispensable as always, Lisa Green was responsible for the overall coordination of the project with all parties involved. To all of them I am forever grateful.

My final and warmest thanks go to Rose Tarlow for her unending support and to my children, Joseph and Ana, for their love and patience during my long sojourns to Los Angeles and my absence from home.

Contents

Preface

It had never occurred to me to write a book about the "making" of a building that I designed. But that was before I became involved with the Getty Center, a project unlike any I had known before, a once-in-a-lifetime commission of such scale, complexity, cost, and ambition that it consumed my life for the better part of fourteen years.

In this case, I thought, the architect's story might be worth telling. Mine is, of course, only one of the stories. The people involved in this vast and exciting project had different responsibilities and, at times, fiercely competing points of view. So many have contributed to this building in a major way that no single book could ever provide an absolutely objective account or do justice to all their invaluable contributions.

For me, the project represented—and, indeed, still does represent—a high point in my career. But it was not lived as a single moment, not the moment I was chosen as the architect or the moment when the design was unveiled or even now as I write this, and the complex is almost complete. Instead, the Getty Center project turned into a long personal and professional journey.

While I was commuting every month to Los Angeles from my home in New York, my children grew up, my hair turned whiter, many friends lost touch with me. And while I continued to work around the world, as I had done for twenty-five years, in Los Angeles I was forced to develop an entirely new approach in my work. The irony did not escape me: I was selected for the Getty on my record—on condition that I broke with my past.

Fortunately, even in moments of dire frustration, my passion for the project never wavered. When I first visited the chaparral-covered site in the mid-1980s; or plowed through the mud of construction in the early 1990s; or walked around the Getty Center shortly before its inauguration, I felt a sense of unimaginable gratification at having been able to design and realize this work. If the cultural campus that now overlooks Los Angeles from a hilltop in Brentwood has come into existence, it is because all those involved—not only the client-trustees, but also innumerable engineers, architects, landscape designers, artists, art historians, and curators, and last but not least the Getty staff—were able to work together to make it happen. I was always certain that we were creating something important, something that would add to the quality of life in Los Angeles, something worthy of the Getty Center's ideals of promoting cultural excellence and making it available to all. And this conviction made it possible for me to remain true to my beliefs as an architect through all the manifold trials of the past fourteen years.

Building the Getty

Chapter 1   Before the Getty

The letter reached me in the first week of October 1983—when exactly I can't tell. It may have lain on my desk in New York for several days while I was flying off to Frankfurt or Atlanta. All I can say for sure is that it caught my attention, as soon as I opened the envelope.

It came from the J. Paul Getty Trust, which at the time was relatively unknown and somewhat esoteric, since it was a new institution and had recently come into vast wealth. Of course I was intrigued. I was being considered along with thirty-two other architects to design a major art-center complex for the Getty Trust in Los Angeles.

Had the trust sent those letters only a few years earlier, I probably would not have been on the list. There was satisfaction just in being included in the selection process because, although I had been a practicing architect since the early 1960s, no one had asked me to work on a large cultural project until 1979.

That was a crucial year for me. It was the time when my firm had been invited along with six others to participate in a competition for the Museum for Decorative Arts in Frankfurt am Main. Although we worked extremely hard on the design, no one could have been more surprised than I when we were awarded first prize: my design was unequivocally modern, and the new museum had to fit into an eighteenth-century context; I was a foreigner, and the museum's collection was an exclusively German cultural legacy; I happened to be Jewish; and most important of all, I had no experience in designing museums.

That Frankfurt commission had been a breakthrough, and a recent one at that. When the letter came from the Getty Trust, I was still busy overseeing construction on the project and on a second, even newer commission, the High Museum of Art in Atlanta. After twenty years of practice, my name was still asssociated with private residences and medium-sized cultural institutions, and I was happy. I felt I was fully engaged in what I had always wanted to do.

Yet I was holding in my hand the letter from the Getty Trust. Of course I would say I was interested—and discover the real meaning of the term "turning point."

I was born in Newark, New Jersey, on October 12, 1934, into a liberal middle-class Jewish family that on my mother's side was engaged in a flourishing tanning business. I could have entered the family business, but I elected to pursue another direction early on. The prospect of becoming an architect appealed to me even before I fully understood what it involved. At Columbia High School in my hometown of Maplewood, New Jersey, I took the usual art history and art courses. Many hours were spent drawing in the basement of our house, where there was an area that I innocently regarded as my "studio." I had a drafting board and often drew or made models of ships, airplanes, and houses. I also used to read magazines like *Architectural Forum* and *House Beautiful* in order to follow the current trends in building design.

One summer, when I was sixteen, I worked for an architect in Newark who was a friend of the family. Though I was just getting coffee, going on errands, and making photocopies of drawings, I began to understand how designs were translated into buildings. The next summer, I worked as an apprentice carpenter-roofer on a suburban housing development. All the houses were the same, but it was thrilling to be building something and to be part of the process of turning blueprints into reality.

When I was applying to colleges, I knew I wanted to study architecture as an undergraduate; this eliminated the possibility of going to Harvard or Yale, since they offered only graduate courses. Instead, I applied to Cornell, the University of Pennsylvania, and MIT. Much to my father's dismay, I chose Cornell, because its courses were more design oriented than those at MIT, which had been my father's alma mater. At Cornell, where I began in 1952, I took courses in painting and art history as well as architecture, and I was exposed to the brilliant teaching of the painter John Hartell and art history professor Alan Solomon. Solomon exercised a lasting influence on me. He later played a radical role as director of the Jewish Museum in New York, where he put on some of the first exhibitions of the work of Jasper Johns and Robert Rauschenberg.

In my final year at Cornell, I designed a house for a professor of government, Arch Dotson, and his wife, Esther. It was a fairly eccentric commission since Dotson had already laid the foundation and I had to design a structure that would fit on top of it. As it happened, the Dotsons wanted more than a conventional house. Since they farmed some of their land, they wanted a studio house, with a sleeping mezzanine, and a large barn attached to one end. The barn was to house a squash court and storage space for agricultural equipment. This ambitious program was somewhat beyond their budget, but the ever ingenious Professor Dotson decided to confront this difficulty by scavenging the remains of Boardman Hall, a 1915 faculty building that was then under demolition. Thus I had the task of installing enormous twelve-foot-high wood-framed windows and beautiful square-foot terra-cotta floor tiles an inch thick. This was my first experience of designing a house as an enormous collage, and in its own strange way it was illuminating.

After graduating from Cornell in 1957, I began an apprenticeship to complete my professional training the following year with Davis, Brody & Wisniewski, which was beginning to establish its reputation as the leading public-housing firm in New York. After one year in this small office with three assistants and three partners, I decided that it was time to set off on a European tour. Taking my portfolio with me in the hope of finding a "finishing" position abroad, I went to Israel, Greece, Italy, France, and Germany, discovering not only the ancient world but also Renaissance and Baroque architecture as well as classical monuments from the nineteenth century. It was, in a sense, my own Grand Tour and a chance to immerse myself in European civilization.

At Cornell, I had studied the great modern architects: Frank Lloyd Wright, Alvar Aalto, and Mies van der Rohe, but the dominant figure for my generation was Charles-Edouard Jeanneret, known as Le Corbusier. Through *Towards a New Architecture* and the collected volumes covering his projected and realized work, his *Oeuvres Complètes*, we all became familiar with the white purist masterpieces of his early career, which we greatly admired. We also came to appreciate the heroic grandeur of his postwar work, usually executed in unfinished, reinforced concrete cast directly from rough timber formwork. In France I visited the 1955 Ronchamp Chapel and the monastery at La Tourette of 1957—both masterpieces of his postwar style. I was drawn to these buildings because of their unique mixture of brutality and delicacy, and the vibrant, changing interior light, particularly dramatic at Ronchamp.

When I left for Europe, I dreamed of working for this renowned Franco-Swiss master. I boldly appeared at 35 rue de Sèvres, his Paris studio, in search of employment, only to be told in no uncertain terms to go away. I was not easily dissuaded, and within a week I returned—but the response was the same. I could not even get past the secretary at the door. Then, some days later I happened to be in the Cité Universitaire just before the Maison du Brésil was to be inaugurated. This building had been designed by Le Corbusier in collaboration with the Brazilian architect Lúcio Costa. The master happened to be there, and I brazenly approached him and on the spot offered to become an unpaid intern in his office. He told me he would never hire an American under any circumstances because, as far as he was concerned, the United States had not only prevented him from being chosen to design the League of Nations building in Geneva in 1927 but also, in the postwar period, from building both the UNESCO building in Paris and the United Nations headquarters in New York. So I left Paris without working for Le Corbusier, but at least I had had the immense satisfaction of coming face-to-face with the great man.

Soon after I tried to find work with the Finnish architect Alvar Aalto, but I was unable to meet him. People in his Helsinki office kept telling me he would be back soon, but after a few days I doubted that he would ever return. The Swiss architect Karl Fleig, who was then the top assistant in Aalto's office, told me: "We haven't heard from him. He just goes off and we don't know where he is, until one day he just reappears." Finally, after visiting all the Aalto architecture I could find in Helsinki and elsewhere in Finland, I decided it was time to return to New York, for by now I had been traveling for six months.

Having failed to find work with a European master, my hope now was to work with Marcel Breuer, the Hungarian-born German Bauhaus architect who had fled to the States in 1937 and who much later became the architect of the Whitney Museum in New York. I had, in fact, written to Breuer from Rome and had been offered a job, which I could not take since I was still traveling. By the time I returned, the job was gone, but, a few weeks later, I was hired by the New York branch of Skidmore, Owings & Merrill, where I worked under Gordon Bunshaft on the Beinecke Rare Book and Manuscript Library at Yale. At that time the Skidmore office was an encouraging and stimulating environment, and I was able to learn how a large corporate office actually functioned. I soon understood that it was organized on a hierarchical basis as a series of smaller offices with a job captain in charge of each one. Bunshaft made a habit of touring the office from one project sector to another, and we junior architects were encouraged to listen in on the dialogue between him and the job captain. One day when I was working on the elevations for the Beinecke Library I happened to tell Bunshaft that I did collages in my spare time. He asked to let him see what I was doing and I eventually did so, whereupon he bought two of them.

Six months later, a position in the Breuer office opened up and I immediately accepted it, feeling at home in a smaller and more intimate environment. Breuer was important to me because I had long admired his work in both Europe and the United States and I felt in need of some kind of rigorous finishing experience. However, Breuer's office was also organized in a pyramidal fashion, with Breuer at the top, three design associates immediately under him, and a team of architects of varying degrees of experience forming the base. I did not have much contact with him, although I worked on a project for a synagogue in New Jersey, which was never built, as well as on a new ski resort for Flaine in France.

While I was in the Breuer office I took up painting and began attending evening classes at the New School for Social Research given by the painter Stephen Greene, who was also teaching at Princeton University. Through Greene I met Frank Stella, who had been his student at Princeton. Since Stephen had already told me that I would do better painting on my own than attending classes, Frank offered me space in his studio. "You can work at night in the studio," he said, "because I'm only there during the day." Stella, who would become a lifelong friend, introduced me to the sculptor Carl Andre and the photographer Hollis Frampton, friends from his Andover days. Andre was already doing minimalist work and moonlighting as a brakeman on a freight train during the day. Hollis was earning his living as a commercial photographer while doing his film projects in the evening. We all worked in Frank's triangular space on West Broadway. As could have been predicted, the studio proved too small, and Frank asked us to move out.

During my second year at Breuer's, I met Michael Graves through a mutual friend who was working with him in the office of George Nelson. We entered a competition together and although we didn't win, this collaboration established our friendship. Since Michael was also painting in his spare time we decided to take a studio together, and in the summer of 1962 we rented space from the painter Philip Pearlstein on East Tenth Street. At that time this street, particularly between Third and Fourth avenues, was effectively the center of the art world in New York. Willem de Kooning had a studio two doors away; one day he poked his head into our room, took a look at the work, and stalked out, presumably in total disgust. This peremptory visit set me thinking. I looked at what I was doing and saw large, rather simplistic gestural Abstract Expressionist paintings in red, white, and blue, while Graves's work consisted of small, subtler palette-knife pieces in dark blues, grays, and browns, bordering on being all but entirely black. I could not speak for Michael, but de Kooning's visit and silent commentary made me realize that I could not possibly hope to succeed as an architect and as a painter. I decided that I had to concentrate on my primary interest and, although I continued to make collages, I stopped making large paintings.

In 1963, toward the end of my three-year apprenticeship with Breuer, I was approached by a young couple from Princeton who had bought a piece of land overlooking the ocean on Fire Island, New York. He was an artist and she a teacher and, while they wanted a beach house, they had only $11,000 to spend. With so little money to work with, I was happy to discover while leafing through a journal that a company in northern Michigan was in the business of producing prefabricated log cabins. The advertisement suggested that they also might be able to produce a more straightforward timber house, and this they agreed to do for the right price. So I submitted the appropriate drawings and had the company precut the entire house. The lumber was shipped by truck and ferry to Fire Island and, in nine days, we managed to erect the house for the allotted sum. I helped with the assembly; we all camped out on the beach and arranged for a local plumber and electrician to install the services. Some ten years later the original owners sold the house for a very handsome profit to Mel Brooks and Anne Bancroft. It was my first freestanding work and I am pleased to say that it's still there.

In the early sixties, working out of my two-room walk-up apartment on Park Avenue and East Ninety-first Street, I managed to obtain some small commissions, including apartment renovations. I also started to teach with Michael Graves at Princeton University and with John Hejduk and Robert Slutzky at Cooper Union. Both Hejduk and Slutzky had previously been part of the so-called Texas Rangers—teaching together with Colin Rowe, Werner Seligmann, and Bernhard Hoesli at the University of Texas at Austin. Slutzky, who studied painting under Josef Albers at Yale University, had been the first one to come from Texas to Cooper Union, and he would be followed shortly by Hejduk, who came expressly to take the position of director of the architectural program at Cooper, which he still holds today, well over thirty years later.

In 1964, my parents had bought an acre of land in Essex Fells, New Jersey, and asked me to design a house for them. Around this time I fell under the spell of Frank Lloyd Wright, and had the good fortune of being invited by Edgar Kaufmann, Jr., to spend a weekend at Wright's Fallingwater House at Mill Run, Pennsylvania. I was overwhelmed by this experience and fascinated by Wright's extension of the interior into the exterior without a break—allowing the fieldstone walls of the house to continue from inside to outside without interruption, except for the steel-framed glazing let directly into the stone. I felt that such an approach was equally applicable to the brick house I was in the process of designing for my parents on a flat New Jersey site, and so I also let the brick walls of my parents' house extend beyond the actual spatial enclosure.

The subsequent publication of the Essex Fells House led to what was to be my first independent commission of any consequence, namely the Smith House, erected on Long Island Sound in Darien, Connecticut, between 1965 and 1967. It was in this house that I began to work in a more consciously complex way with interpenetrating spaces and transparency, partially influenced by the Rowe and Slutzky distinction between literal and phenomenal transparency. These attributes have been an integral part of my architecture ever since. This was also my first white building, although it was in fact faced quite traditionally with vertical wood siding painted white. Little did I imagine that I would later become known as the "white" architect. Then it just seemed to be the natural thing to do. New England clapboard houses are invariably painted white and the Smith House, being of the same material, was treated in exactly the same way. However, spatially speaking, it could hardly have been more different.

Now I often wonder how it is that my architecture came to acquire what for many people is its singular style: this image of a perennially gleaming white building flooded with light. Like many other architects, I suppose, I can only counter this perception of a seemingly unified "house style" by saying that I have been subject to many influences over the years—not only modern architects like Le Corbusier, Frank Lloyd Wright, Mies van der Rohe, and Louis Kahn but also traditional masters within the European humanistic tradition, like Bernini, Borromini, and Bramante, and above all the less well-known architect Balthasar Neumann. Even with this grounding in tradition, I have always followed the modernist line but, despite my fondness for the work of Le Corbusier, I have done so without adhering to any particular style. My infamous "white" manner has simply evolved out of an overriding preference for planar, spatial assemblies and for contrapuntal interplay between solid and void, between free-form and geometrical structure, and, above all I suppose, for the unification of fluid space through large glazed planes. I have always been preoccupied with the filtration and reflection of natural light, with chiaroscuro effects, and with the way in which a building becomes animated through the movement of the subject in space. While I would consider my own style to be "classically" modernist, the whiteness of my work often has been regarded as aggressive, forbidding, and altogether too severe. For me, however, white has always been a source of tranquillity because it brings objects and color into sharp focus. It also dramatically reflects the changing light of a day.

In 1964 I met up again with Peter Eisenman, who had been a year ahead of me at Cornell and had just returned from teaching at Cambridge University in England. That year I joined him along with Michael Graves, Charles Gwathmey, and John Hejduk in forming the CASE group, an acronym for the somewhat preposterous title Committee of Architects for the Study of the Environment. This group first met in the fall of 1964 in the grand Lowrie House at Princeton University. Conceived by Eisenman as a kind of American equivalent to the prewar European Congrès Internationaux d'Architecture Moderne, this group initially embraced a rather wide spectrum of East Coast architects and intellectuals including Robert Venturi and Tim Vreeland from Philadelphia, Giovanni Pasanella and Jacquelin Robertson from New York, Stanford Anderson and Henry Millon from MIT, Colin Rowe from Cornell University, and Vincent Scully from Yale. Also included were John Hejduk and Robert Slutzky as the representatives from Cooper Union and Michael McKinnell of Kallman/McKinnell, who had just won the competition for the Boston city hall. Kenneth Frampton, who was then technical editor of the British magazine *Architectural Design*, was flown over for this extravagant weekend event, and we shared an enormous bedroom in Lowrie House, each in his separate damask-draped four-poster bed, surrounded by large Chinese jars and other priceless knickknacks.

The ultimate result of this intellectual jamboree was further position papers and endless arcane discussions at subsequent meetings and, above all, a seminar held in 1969 at the Museum of Modern Art in New York under the patronage of Arthur Drexler, when Eisenman, Graves, Gwathmey, Hejduk, and I presented our current projects and Rowe and Frampton engaged in a formal critique of our work. The proceedings of this event were published by George Wittenborn in 1972 as *Five Architects*. This book established us as a loose association of young architects and provoked considerable discussion in international architecture circles. The work portrayed in *Five Architects* was seen in part as a critical response to the modern "vernacular" school represented by the work of Robert Venturi, as this had been theoretically elaborated by him in his 1966 Museum of Modern Art publication, *Complexity and Contradiction in Architecture*. The ensuing polemics between the purist "whites" and the pragmatic "grays" would later be matched by the even fiercer confrontation between modernism and postmodernism in the late 1970s in which I would acquire new enemies by dismissing postmodernism as meaningless pastiche. Looking back, it seems that, then as now, the rigorously abstract, mostly white architecture of *Five Architects* was seen as totally antithetical to American values and above all to the domestic comfort of suburban life. In 1967 Eisenman, in collaboration with Arthur Drexler of MoMA, founded the Institute for Architecture and Urban Studies in New York, and for the next fifteen years this institution and its magazine, *Oppositions*, would be the center of architectural debate in the United States. We would all congregate there in the evenings for lectures and exhibitions. It had the aura of a heroic and polemically creative place.

The Smith House was featured in a number of architectural magazines, and it led to further commissions to build private homes. One day I received a letter from a Mr. and Mrs. James Douglas inquiring if I would sell them the blueprints for the Smith House. I replied that while I was not prepared to sell the drawings I would certainly be willing to design a totally new house for them along similar lines. They accepted, and I started designing a house for a site that they had purchased in a subdivision in northern Michigan. As it happened, the builder-developer who had sponsored the subdivision insisted on reviewing the design of any house that would be built within its boundary. He asked me to submit photographs of my work, whereupon he immediately refused to permit a house designed by me since it did not have the prerequisite pitched roof and so on. To my delight, the Douglases responded to this impasse by promptly selling the plot and looking for another site. They fortunately found one, on top of a steeply wooded cliff face overlooking Lake

Michigan, and it was for this spot that I had the pleasure of designing a much more spectacular house for them. This house, when completed, attracted considerable attention, receiving an honor award from the American Institute of Architects. These domestic commissions enabled me to experiment with different spatial relations and to expand the syntax of my architecture. Since all these houses were on isolated, bucolic sites, I learned to develop a very intimate connection between each building and its immediate natural environment.

Earlier, in 1967, while still working on relatively small private commissions, I was invited by the J. M. Kaplan Fund, in association with the National Endowment for the Arts, to convert the Bell Telephone Laboratory complex in Greenwich Village into low-cost housing and studios for artists. Westbeth was a pioneering experience since, at the time, it was the largest adaptive reuse project in the world, creating some four hundred residences and studios for artists. It also provided subsidized communal studio spaces for the Merce Cunningham Dance Company and Ellen Stewart's experimental theater, La Mama.

In the late 1960s, the New York State Urban Development Corporation asked me to design a public housing project in the Bronx, Twin Parks Northeast. This was made up of three mid-rise housing blocks of an irregular shape that responded to the complex street configuration surrounding the site. Involving a total of two hundred new apartments, this was my second collective-housing commission, and in effect my first effort to create a new apartment type for low-income families. In both projects, the creation of communal outdoor space was an integral part of the overall concept, although Twin Parks was my first entirely new work in a strictly urban context. I used dark-colored masonry in order to integrate the mid-rise blocks into the adjacent low-rise brownstone fabric. The project was completed successfully, but the experience proved to be disheartening. Although these buildings still stand, their interiors have been ravaged, and urban social conditions prevailing today have become so brutal and dangerous that the plaza is now fenced off in order to provide security for residents.

Looking back, I now realize that the public housing experiment of this period—using respected architects and providing adequate funds—was unique. In those days, we naively took it for granted and it is nothing short of disastrous that housing of this order is no longer being provided. We should not forget that the original agenda of the modern movement was to design public works such as housing schemes, hospitals, and schools for the social benefit of all. It is a sad fact that since the late 1970s, architects have been largely reduced to serving the private sector.

In 1970, before welfare programs came to an abrupt end in the New York region, I was fortunate enough to be commissioned to design the Bronx Developmental Center, a large residential and treatment center for mentally and physically disabled children. Built for the New York State Department of Mental Health, the Bronx Developmental Center accommodated some 380 children as permanent residents, and also included an extensive outpatient facility. Its common features included a beautifully furnished indoor swimming pool for paraplegics and a generous assembly hall. Carefully laid out on a landscaped, triangular site in a blighted industrial area, it was my most elaborate public work to date. Aside from its aim to be perceived as a city-in-miniature, it was also extremely ambitious technically since we pioneered here a new system of aluminum sandwich panel cladding.

Ever since my first extended trip abroad, following my graduation from Cornell, I had felt very drawn to European culture. In 1973 I was invited to become resident architect at the American Academy in Rome, and in accepting this position I wanted to benefit not only from studying the architecture of Rome but also, as Louis Kahn had done before me, by taking fellow scholars of the academy on study trips elsewhere in Europe. I was particularly fascinated by the Roman sites and hilltop towns, which had achieved a sense of permanence on their dramatic terrain. To experience the color and texture of Italy's cultural heritage remains an indispensable aspect of any architect's education. Little did I imagine at the time that this intense experience of the monuments and gardens of Italy would later have a major impact on my conception of the Getty Center, as did a study tour that I made of Baroque churches in southern Germany at the end of my time at the academy.

Even before my stay there, I realized that the civic museum had become the surrogate cathedral of our time. Yet, it had never occurred to me before how much a city like Rome could also serve as a vast museum, while still being an everyday urban experience. This seemed to be an ideal state of affairs, one that could compensate for the isolation of many modern museums. I saw how a museum could be used to influence the existing urban fabric, just as the cathedral and its *parvis* had in earlier times.

In 1975, shortly before the Bronx Developmental Center was completed, I was commissioned to design a new visitors center for the historic village of New Harmony in Indiana. This village had come into being in 1814, when George Rapp founded the Harmony Society as an ideal community. Rapp provided his earliest followers with a so-called boatload of knowledge—a substantial library that he had accumulated and that was shipped to them on the banks of the Wabash River. Later, in 1825, the socialist reformer Robert Owen had reorganized the community as an experiment in socialist living. It was to have been housed in a monastic structure designed by the English architect Stedman Whitwell. While this ambitious utopian compound was never realized, I was inspired by Whitwell's vision. Since I could not match such a concept within the confines of a small visitors center, I conceived of the building's form as an abstract metaphor for the original "boatload of knowledge." I treated the new Atheneum as a kind of grounded boat raised up above the flood-plain of the river. From this artificial vantage point I tried to open up the building on all sides to sweeping views of the surrounding countryside and to evoke this topography by means of a ramped system of circulation that rose to the top of the building. The building also acquired a peculiarly organic quality by responding through its geometry to the grid of the town on one side and the curvilinear form of the river on the other.

The year 1977 was a momentous year for me in many ways, for not only was the Atheneum under construction but I was working on the New York School Exhibition at the State Museum in Albany and on the Aye Simon Reading Room in the Guggenheim Museum. More important, I was serving as a visiting professor at the Graduate School of Design at Harvard University, where I met my future wife, Katherine Gormley, who was then a student at the school. Two years later, when the Atheneum was inaugurated, our first child, Joseph, was born.

While I was still involved with the Atheneum, I was selected as architect for the Hartford Seminary, a theological center in the inner suburbs of Hartford, Connecticut. The seminary, which enabled me to expand on the public character of the Atheneum commission, included a library, a large meeting room, classrooms, and a chapel, this last being incorporated into the program at my suggestion. The seminary had a dual personality, which had to be reflected in the design: it had to afford a scholarly and introspective atmosphere, and it had also to make some of its facilities available to the general public.

It was at this fateful moment in 1979 that I was invited to participate in the competition for the Museum for Decorative Arts in Frankfurt am Main. The other competitors were my compatriot Robert Venturi, my friend Hans Hollein from Vienna (both of whom eventually received second prizes), the Czech practice of Novotny and Mäher, and three German offices: Heinz Mohl, Holzinger & Goepfert, and Trint & Quasi. There is no doubt in my mind that this prestigious commission presaged the involvement of other foreign architects in German competitions and building projects.

While our design for the museum was uncompromisingly radical, it was also carefully inscribed into the existing context. Above all, it took into consideration the character of the riverfront site following the course of the Main, and also responded very directly to the elegant cubic form of the existing eighteenth-century Villa Metzler poised on the edge of the Schaumainkai. Since we had to incorporate this existing building into our design, the new museum derived its proportions from the 17.6-cubic-meter mass of the villa. Our new building was made up of three comparable cubic pavilions set at each of the remaining three corners. A rotated asymmetrical courtyard was inserted into the center of the complex; this enabled us to establish the main axis of the building, which was eventually extended into the landscape of the adjacent park. A glazed bridge formed the link between the new museum and the Villa Metzler, while the new gallery sequence was given energy by the glazed ramp and stairway. Departing from the traditional way of presenting decorative art, I was able to design large built-in display settings to show the collection in a contemporary way.

The design of the Frankfurt museum led to my commission to design the High Museum of Art in Atlanta, Georgia, in 1980. I had only the design drawings and the model of Frankfurt to show the selection committee, but its members were persuaded that I was capable of responding to the civic and cultural demands of the program. So, between 1980 and 1983, I found myself traveling between two cities that were some four thousand miles apart and working on museums involving very different cultures, clients, collections, and physical environments. While the cities were almost the same size, the character of their cultural heritage could hardly be compared. The Museum for Decorative Arts is just one of fifteen museums in Frankfurt, whereas in Atlanta the High Museum is a major institution for all of the visual arts.

In the High Museum, I paid tribute to Frank Lloyd Wright's Guggenheim Museum by designing ramped systems of circulation in a quadrant around a top-lit atrium. Since this central space was conceived as an indoor public plaza, it was hoped that the atrium of the High Museum, like the core of Wright's Guggenheim, would be used for civic events, such as concerts and theatrical performances, and this is exactly what happened. Unlike the Guggenheim's spiral, the High's ramped promenade carries visitors between flat floors, while offering framed views of the exterior. The works of art themselves are displayed in horizontal galleries, conceived as self-contained and intimate spaces. As before, I tried to evoke a feeling of freedom by allowing natural light to enter the atrium as far as this was compatible with the display of art.

If anything distinguishes my public buildings, it is the way they are designed to fit into the existing pedestrian routes of a city. In the case of the immense City Hall and Library in The Hague, in the Netherlands, which I designed in 1986 and which took almost a decade to complete because of complex political machinations, an eleven-story-high glass-covered atrium—open at both ends to the street—helps reassure visitors that they are not going to be trapped in a bureaucratic labyrinth. Instead of losing themselves in miles of corridors, they can readily identify their appointed destinations as soon as they enter the galleria. Even on gray days, this vast atrium is flooded with natural light, which enlivens the environment not only for visitors but also for the employees whose offices flank both sides of the space.

Chapter 2　Selecting the Architect

When J. Paul Getty died in 1976, the museum in Malibu that carries his name housed his priceless collection of Greek and Roman antiquities, as well as a substantial collection of Renaissance and Baroque painting and eighteenth-century French decorative art. However, this was not to be the oil magnate's principal cultural legacy—for, at his death, he bequeathed a considerable quantity of Getty Oil stock to the museum, stock that in 1982 became the $700 million endowment of the J. Paul Getty Trust.

When the endowment was first made available, it was accompanied by the legal requirement that 4.25 percent be spent annually on art-related projects. The trustees immediately began studying how best to administer these extraordinary new resources. By 1981, when Harold M. Williams, a former chairman of the U.S. Securities and Exchange Commission, was appointed the new president of the Getty Trust, a number of ambitious plans had begun to be formulated. Apart from continuing to expand the museum's collection along the lines established by J. Paul Getty, the trustees realized that they could do more to promote the study of art. They saw that the trust could create new programs related to art history, conservation, education, and museum management, as well as provide grants to outside art institutions and scholars for projects of research and conservation in the various arts. It was also decided to expand the trust's public role. Beyond creating a museum with the usual range of ancillary facilities, the trust felt that it should establish a unique world-class institution in art and cultural research.

With Texaco's acquisition of Getty Oil in 1983, the original $700 million endowment soared to $1.7 billion, a windfall that encouraged the trustees to rethink their overall program along even more ambitious lines. To this end, the trust purchased a 110-acre hilltop site in West Los Angeles with the intention of building an art center covering some twenty-four acres of the site. Initially, the project was restricted to a major art museum plus the quarters that were necessary to house the trust's new activities.

For me, the process began with a letter, dated September 30, 1983, from Bill N. Lacy, who was then the architectural adviser of the selection committee. It stated that the estimated cost of this project was between $75 million and $100 million. We were told that thirty-three internationally known architects were being invited to submit materials to the committee and that six of those firms would then be selected to visit the site and meet with the committee. The penultimate phase would be the recommendation of three firms to the president of the Getty Trust, in unranked order, for his consideration and subsequent presentation to the board.

On October 25, 1983, I replied, indicating that I intended to submit our credentials for consideration. A few days later, on November 1, I sent the committee the relevant material and expanded in brief on my general approach:

> The design of the Getty Art Complex poses a tremendous challenge to the architect. As a unique museological, cultural, and educational facility, it will have a major impact on the cultural life not only of California but of the entire country and the world. We also recognize that as the premier undertaking of the J. Paul Getty Trust it will represent an extraordinary commitment on the part of

the trust to excellence in both art history and architecture. The prospect of bringing our special talents and experience to such an assignment is extremely exciting, and we feel that our capabilities are uniquely suited to the challenge. All of our work is based on a philosophy which integrates aesthetics, context, and function into a contemporary vision of architecture that is both spirited—in all senses of the word—and humane.

Although I had had little time to think about the project and had only the vaguest inkling of what the trust desired, I entered the selection process with great enthusiasm. My submission included photographs and graphic documentation of the High Museum in Atlanta and the Museum for Decorative Arts in Frankfurt, together with similar data on the Atheneum in New Harmony and the Hartford Seminary in Connecticut and information on two smaller projects. I wanted to illustrate clearly the range of our experience in dealing with museums and similar public programs.

Aside from Lacy, the selection committee was made up of Reyner P. Banham, Chair, Department of Art History, University of California, Santa Cruz; Richard Bender, Chair, College of Environmental Design, University of California, Berkeley; Kenneth Dayton, Chair, Executive Committee, Dayton-Hudson Corporation, and former member of the National Council on the Arts; Anne d'Harnoncourt, Director, Philadelphia Museum of Art; Ada Louise Huxtable, former architecture critic for *The New York Times;* and Craig Hugh Smyth, former Director, I Tatti, Florence, and former Director, Institute of Fine Arts, New York University. In addition, Harold Williams and Nancy Englander, representing the Getty Trust, participated as non-voting members. The committee responded quickly and on November 23, 1983, Bill Lacy notified me that our firm had been chosen for further consideration, which meant that the committee members would consult some of my former clients and visit a number of my completed projects early in 1984. Lacy went on to indicate that I would be called to Los Angeles for an interview with the entire committee sometime toward the end of January.

Lacy's letter did not reveal that the initial list of thirty-three firms had now been reduced to seven (not six as originally expected), but I later learned that I was being considered along with I. M. Pei & Partners; Batey & Mack; Venturi, Rauch and Scott Brown; James Stirling, Michael Wilford and Associates; Fumihiko Maki and Associates; and Mitchell/Giurgola. All were established architects, but the list struck me as a little odd, since it represented such divergent architectural and philosophical positions. I found it difficult to understand how the committee could possibly consider Venturi's "honky-tonk" populism and Stirling's late neoclassical modernism as being equally appropriate for the Getty Center, as say, I. M. Pei's corporate manner or my own neo-purist approach: how could it contemplate under the same rubric a young hip practice like Batey & Mack and a practitioner as seasoned and as precise as Maki? It was impossible to guess what kind of architect the trust was looking for. Moreover, in retrospect, I find it surprising that only two foreign architects were included on the shortlist.

Around that time, I had a conversation with Richard Bender, a member of the selection committee. While he maintained the necessary discretion, he indicated the range of issues that would interest the committee. This helped me to focus on the distinguishing features of the project—notably, the importance of the site, southern California's special climate and light, and the need for a building that would stand the test of time. Since I had never designed a building on the West Coast before, it had already occurred to me that I would have to find an appropriate approach to form in order to respond fully to the uniqueness of the climate.

It was a while before I would be able to present my ideas to the committee. Even before we went on the obligatory tour of my previous work. I was aware of unease among certain members of the committee about my abstract modernist approach. Faced with my known preference for naturally lit modern spaces, they did not hesitate to indicate that they favored underlit gallery volumes combined with a period setting for much of the collection.

Early in 1984, committee members began touring the major projects of the short-listed architects, including, in my case, the High Museum in Atlanta, the Atheneum in New Harmony, and the Museum for Decorative

Arts in Frankfurt. They obviously had a great deal of ground to cover, and their visits, at least to Atlanta and New Harmony, were somewhat rushed. Still, I was able to accompany them and I used the visits to emphasize points that I imagined might be relevant to the Getty Center.

A chance to explain my ideas more fully came on April 19, 1984, when the other candidates and I were invited to address the committee in Los Angeles. In the interim, I received a letter from Lacy dated March 27 in which he noted that John Walsh and Kurt Forster had been appointed as key directors of the future Getty Center and would from now on be sitting on the selection committee. He also enclosed the initial draft program for the new J. Paul Getty Fine Arts Center.

At that point, the program comprised only three elements: the Center for the History of Art and the Humanities (later to be renamed the Research Institute for the History of Art and the Humanities); the Conservation Institute; and the museum. In addition, the draft program specified that the campus would have a self-contained auditorium capable of seating five hundred to six hundred people as well as other smaller meeting rooms. The Center for the History of Art and the Humanities, which had only just been created and was housed temporarily in Santa Monica, would contain a world-class library and a photographic archive of works of art as well as research accommodation for twenty to forty international scholars at any one time. The equally new Conservation Institute, which was then based in Marina del Rey, would aim to give the Getty an international presence by using the latest scientific techniques to restore artistic treasures around the world. Finally, the new museum was to house the Getty collection of paintings, drawings, decorative arts, and illuminated manuscripts, but not the Greek and Roman collections, which would remain in Malibu. We were further informed that the new museum would allow for expansion of the collection and accommodation of temporary exhibitions.

In explaining the interview procedure, Lacy informed us that we would each meet with the committee and other non-voting observers for ninety minutes, with a further thirty minutes set aside for *in camera* discussions of each candidate. The committee did not want to see more slides, photographs, or sketches of previous work or even specific proposals for the new complex. Rather, the interview was to be entirely conversational. We were each accorded about an hour in which to make our presentations, with the remainder of our allotted time given over to questions and answers.

It is interesting to note that, at this time, the Getty evidently had little idea of the eventual size, scope, and cost of the undertaking. In Lacy's March 27, 1984, letter he noted that there had been no major changes in the site that would materially affect the design of the project, even though an additional parcel of 600 acres had in fact been acquired to the north of the original 110-acre site. While remarking that this additional land was intended as a future preserve, he went on to emphasize that the original 110 acres already had planning approval for thirty-five single-family detached houses and that a rezoning application for the Getty project was in process. Somewhat ominously, he added that preliminary estimates called for approximately the same site coverage by the proposed center as existed for the earlier residential scheme.

I went to Los Angeles a few days before the interview, eager to familiarize myself with both the site and its surroundings. Although I had been there before, it was not a city that I knew at all well. I was surprised once again by its size and, above all, by its primarily suburban character. Coming from New York, I was struck by the lack of any readily discernible center. Of course I was aware of the names of the well-known neighborhoods—Beverly Hills, Bel Air, Hollywood, Santa Monica, Brentwood—but I could not place them in relationship to each other. I remember thinking grandly that Sunset Boulevard in Santa Monica stood exactly at the other end of the sun's trajectory from what for me was its more familiar rising along Sunrise Highway in Montauk, Long Island. It was as if the sun's voyage across the United States confirmed California's status as the last American frontier.

Irrespective of such idle musings, everything seemed strangely transient. Where Sunset Boulevard meets the Pacific, I hoped to see something dramatic, some sort of celebration that would announce to latter-day transcontinental migrants that they had reached their destination. Instead, there was only Gladstone's 4 Fish, a modest restaurant specializing in local seafood. I could not help thinking that perhaps one day the Getty Center would serve as a more appropriate conclusion to this symbolic axis.

I visited the Getty Museum in Malibu and found its collection to be of great interest, but I felt the conflation of Greek and Roman art, the collection of European painting and sculpture drawn largely from the fifteenth to the nineteenth centuries, plus a decorative-arts collection mainly devoted to eighteenth-century French furniture displayed in period rooms was an eccentric and oddly disjunctive combination. In addition, the building itself, a reincarnation of the Villa dei Papiri near Herculaneum, which was buried when Mount Vesuvius erupted in A.D. 79, conveyed a pleasant archaeological but unreal atmosphere. Apart from the fact that this reconstruction had been based on fragmentary evidence as to the original scope and size of the Roman villa, the aura of this archaic simulation was seriously compromised by the fact that one could gain access to its spectacular courtyard garden facing the sea only by passing through a hollow, cavernous podium–cum–parking garage situated immediately underneath. As I wandered around the upper level, however, other aspects of the museum appealed to me—notably the courtyard spaces, the feeling of openness, and the direct relationship of the gallery space to the garden. I still believe that the uniqueness of this museum stems from its intimate scale as well as the free movement of people between inside and outside that is so well suited to both the climate and the site. In Los Angeles, the light seems to reach every corner of the landscape; when I first visited the site of the future Getty Center, on a beautiful day with unusually good visibility, I immediately understood that light and space were central to the California experience.

I found the site remarkably unspoiled. It covered the top of a hill that dropped sharply to the east toward the San Diego Freeway and sloped more gently to the west toward the shaded, luxurious homes of Brentwood. After its trees were destroyed in the 1961 Bel Air fire, which jumped the freeway, it had become overgrown with chaparral and was filled with wildlife of extremely varied kinds: deer, snakes, coyotes, foxes, and innumerable birds. The previous owner had turned to viticulture after selling the site to the Getty. He had had a hobby of driving golf balls into the wilderness from a little plateau that he had constructed on the crest of the hill. When I came to live on the site and fell into the daily routine of walking over the area, I eventually found more than a hundred golf balls that he had scattered all over the terrain. The landform itself had no great natural beauty, but the movement of the contours was extremely vivacious, and the views afforded by different vantage points were unquestionably spectacular.

Walking along little footpaths through the undergrowth the first time, I made my way over undulating land to a high point that stood like a promontory at the southern end of the site. From here, I looked east toward the San Gabriel Mountains, south toward Los Angeles, and west toward Santa Monica and the Pacific Ocean. On the rest of the site, these views were obscured by the chaparral, but I noticed this had one advantage. Where I could not see the freeway, I could not hear it, so it was possible to be in the open air and still enjoy relative silence. I made a mental note of this, since I wanted visitors to the Center to be able to move in and out of buildings without being constantly aware of the city below.

At my interview with the selection committee on April 19, 1984, I made my presentation as though it were a lecture, improvising as I went along but using notes for guidance. I began by talking about my experience as an architect working in both Europe and America and went on to say how I felt one ought to combine the European ideal of permanence and feeling for history with American attitudes of openness, flexibility, and invention. I further spoke of my reaction to the city of Los Angeles, to its spatial quality, its sky, its climate, and its light, all of which seemed to offer rich creative possibilities.

I advanced the idea of the museum as a vehicle for "collective memory," as an institution that encompasses inspiration and enchantment. While it was clear to me that the museum would be the most important building on the site, it would be only one of a number that would have to relate to each other and to the topography. I already imagined a horizontal layering of spaces, interconnected around courtyards on different levels. I spoke of rooms of various sizes, which would be open to the landscape as well as to a series of interior and exterior spaces. I referred to the Roman use of stone and its sense of permanence. I cited Hadrian's

Villa as a museological paradigm: a collection of antique fragments cradled in the midst of a wild and picturesque nature. I was already aware that the trustees were concerned about building a center that was too monumental and ostentatious in its overall appearance. Yet, given the nature of the site, a citadel-like character was almost inevitable, as was the analogy to a Tuscan hill town. Irrespective of the topographic image invoked, I felt that the Center should not appear to be apologizing for itself. I thought that above all it must convey the confidence and idealism appropriate to an institution devoted to the promotion of the arts. Finally, I pledged that, if chosen, I would dedicate all my energies to the project.

The question-and-answer period that followed went over some of the same ground. The committee showed little interest in knowing more about my earlier projects or even in learning more about my early ideas concerning the new project. Rather, we talked about less tangible things, such as how my work related to the history of architecture or how I might deal with the different, sometimes conflicting, practical concerns of the client. After that, the committee went into closed session and I returned to New York to await its decision, which I optimistically hoped would lead me to the next stage of this all-consuming project.

Four days later, on April 23, 1984, I received a telegram from Bill Lacy informing me that I had made it to the final shortlist along with Fumihiko Maki and James Stirling. He congratulated me on behalf of the committee and conveyed, with faultless decorum, how much they appreciated the opportunity to become more familiar with my work. He told me that I would soon be briefed on the next steps in the selection process.

There appeared to be a certain logic in the committee's choice of the three architects: we were all producing distinguished work that still adhered to the modern tradition, and we had each designed a significant museum that had recently been built. The British architect Stirling had just finished the Neue Staatsgalerie in Stuttgart, Maki had just completed the Iwasaki Art Museum in Ibusuki, Japan, and I had recently realized the High Museum, and the Museum for Decorative Arts in Frankfurt. I did not know Maki at that time, but Stirling was an old friend who used to spend weekends in my New York apartment when he was teaching at Yale during the late 1960s and 1970s. We were to remain firm friends throughout his life despite the fact that on this occasion we were rivals. Although Jim was an outspoken member of the British New Brutalist movement, he had always supported my work, and he reacted with his typical warmth and generosity when I was finally selected.

For the next stage, Lacy's original selection committee was disbanded and a new committee, headed by Harold Williams, was formed to make the final appointment. This committee was also eager to visit the short-listed architects' recent work, which, in my case, meant going again to the museums in Atlanta and Frankfurt, as well as to the Hartford Seminary. The new committee had as its members Harold Williams, who was the president and chief executive officer of the trust; Nancy Englander, who was still in charge of program analysis; John Walsh, who had been appointed museum director in October 1983; Kurt Forster, recently appointed director of the Center for the History of Art and the Humanities; Bill Lacy, who continued to serve as architectural adviser; and John Fey, Jon Lovelace, Rocco Siciliano, and J. Patrick Whaley, who were all members of the board of trustees. I was soon to become familiar with the members of this new committee since, after their appointment, we spent time together in Frankfurt and elsewhere.

In early May, soon after I was selected as one of the three Getty finalists, I had the delightful surprise of being awarded the Pritzker Architecture Prize, which by then had already become popularly known as the Nobel Prize for architecture. I was totally overwhelmed because I did not even know that I was being considered. It was a great honor, not least because at the age of forty-nine I was the youngest recipient to date. Philip Johnson, Luis Barragán, James Stirling, Kevin Roche, and I. M. Pei had been its recipients in the past. It was unclear to me how the prize would affect the decision of the Getty selection committee, although it could hardly be a liability.

The period between April and October 1984 was unsettling. For a time, I was beset by anxiety mixed with restrained expectation. At the same time I was kept extremely busy, not only with overseeing the completion of the Frankfurt museum but also with designing an addition to the Des Moines Art Center and preparing to enter another competition to build a new headquarters for Siemens in Munich. Despite all this activity the Getty selection process was constantly on my mind. Architectural journals were running articles speculating over who might finally be selected. I seemed to be continually giving committee members tours of my museums, receiving them in my New York office, and answering endless questions. The selection committee was kept equally busy visiting buildings in the United States, Europe, and Japan.

I slowly was getting to know each of the committee members, in particular Harold Williams, Nancy Englander, John Walsh, and Kurt Forster. It was during this early process that I was made once again aware that certain committee members were worried about the "whiteness" of my architecture. I had maintained all along that, if chosen to design the Getty Center, I would be sensitive to the need for an appropriate material, suitable both to the site and to the character of the institution. While reassuring them that the complex did not have to be white, I still stated my preference for using a self-cleansing membrane paneled in enameled metal since this, as I had demonstrated elsewhere, was a peerless technique with which one could readily achieve a fluid transition between orthogonal and curved elements.

At Lacy's insistence, I agreed to write an account of my overall approach to the design of the complex, with particular attention to the use of materials. I elaborated on positions that I had already expounded in previous interviews, and although he had asked for only a brief statement, I ended up sending a four-page letter. It was perhaps the closest I had come to fully articulating in writing my position as an architect. While acknowledging my past preference for whiteness, I emphasized the need for a different use of materials that would create a permanent and solid profile along the crest of the hill. The date was October 12, 1984, which happened to be my fiftieth birthday. Since this was the first time I would write a complete account of my approach to the design of the Getty, I have decided to quote it here in full:

Dear Bill:

In response to your letter, I would like to make the following comments about my approach to the use of materials in the J. Paul Getty Trust Art Complex. Architecture is an art of substance, of materialized ideas about space. Between the demands of program, site, locale, and building technology, the architect has to find a means of making buildings communicate in the language of materials and textures. Buildings are for the contemplation of the eyes and the mind, but also, no less importantly, to be experienced and savored by all the human senses. You cannot have form in architecture which is unrelated to human experience; and you cannot approach an understanding of experience, in terms of architecture, without a strongly sensuous and tactile attitude toward form and space. The spectacular site of the Getty Complex invites the architect to search out a precise and natural topography. This implies a harmony of parts; a rational procedure; concern for qualities of proportion, rhythm, and response; precision of detail, constructional integrity, programmatic appropriateness; and, not least, a respect for human scale. All of these issues relate intimately to the choice of materials.

The material elements of the complex—the composition and character of masses, textures, volumes—must, in fact, be determined by specific, sensitive reactions to the site and by topological responses derived from the programmatic requirements. At the same time, the unity of the whole complex must also be ensured by a governing conceptual idea regarding the usage of materials. This concept may be derived from a basic idea of the complementarity relationship between built form and natural form, something which may be seen in all of my previous work. This relationship of complementarity does not so much imply opposition as harmony and balance.

Besides its topography, the most powerful aspect of the Getty site is the quality of the light that is natural to it, which is astonishingly beautiful. That clear, golden California light is, I must say, intoxicating to an Easterner. I long to make walls that have openings for the glorious light to flood through, casting crisp, delicious shadows. I am eager to see built structures set against that brilliant blue sky of southern California. I can envisage a complex based on a horizontal layering of spaces, interconnected around courtyards on different levels, large and small rooms opening out to the landscape, a series of interior and exterior spaces that relate both to the site and to the nature of the collection.

Besides this American attitude of openness, warmth, flexibility, and invention, my vision of the building also has to do with a more European-derived ideal of permanence, specificity, and history. The materials used should reaffirm this image of solidity, of permanent presence in the landscape. Architecture at its best is an integration of human scale with civic grandeur, decorative simplicity with material richness, an interest in technical innovation with respect for historical precedent. Thus, I can envision a complex made up of larger volumetric pieces counterpointed by smaller elements made of materials that lend themselves to light, delicate framelike structures. The volumetric pieces would probably be constructed of materials that are massive, make for permanent anchoring, and are solid and rocklike in appearance, stable, long-lived. One thinks of various cut stones, such as granite (smooth and rough textured), travertine, marble, sandstone, limestone. Stone could be used in large-scale and small-scale blocks, on both vertical and horizontal surfaces, its sizes and textures juxtaposed in order to play off intimate surfaces against more massive ones.

The counterpoint to the stone elements in the complex would be likely to include materials such as aluminum, bronze, nickel-plated or stainless-steel surface treatments or structural components, as well as many kinds of glazing. All of these would, of course, have to be compatible with the southern California climate. Thus we imagine a dialogue: a massive enclosure, but also open, lightweight, transparent glazed areas.

But once again, it's not just a matter of opposites—there must be a balance that is related to the site, to the contours and history of the land, to the program, as well as to the plasticity of the whole composition. I am also thinking about the beautiful effect of long, massive expanses of whitewashed stucco walls such as one sees in many Spanish Colonial buildings. This may be something we would also like to strive to capture here, whether in stucco itself or in some more refined material with analogous properties of texture and density. We can envision using a material of this kind in some of the more domestically scaled, intimate spaces that have an informal character, but still demand a classic material expression.

Naturally, the scope of the materials selected and the colors integrally implied by those materials have to be determined by the relationship between all finishes and components. This means that one must look at the whole, while also remaining sensitive to even the smallest-scale building element, from copings, roofing materials, skylights, hardware, and mechanical and electrical devices to landscape elements and outdoor furniture.

When we address the issue of interior materials (and we are thinking now specifically of the museum component of the program), the most important aspect is that the objects within the collections should emerge as the major protagonists of the space. Therefore, the choice of wall, floor, and ceiling surfaces will have to vary according to the contents of the rooms. This means that all backdrops need not necessarily be painted plaster walls, but may be materials derived more carefully from scale considerations, the "ambiance" or atmosphere one wishes to create, and the comfort and appeal to the museumgoer of a variety of different surface treatments. These could include such hard and soft materials as wood and fabric.

Naturally, the treatment of the interior is related to that of the exterior and integral to the architectural conception as a whole; in both there must be a paramount concern for materials that age well and function well. Finally, I should emphasize my belief that all materials ought to be studied on the site and under natural conditions of light and coloration. Extensive sample and test panels should be erected and full-scale models of room interiors built. Nothing should be finalized until such on-site experiments have been studied and discussed.

In my mind's eye, I see a classic structure, elegant and timeless, emerging, serene and ideal, from the rough hillside, a kind of Aristotelian structure within the landscape. Sometimes I think that the landscape overtakes it, and sometimes I see the structure as standing out, dominating the landscape. The two are entwined in a dialogue, a perpetual embrace in which building and site are one. In my mind, I keep returning to the Romans—to Hadrian's Villa, to Caprarola—for their sequences, their spaces, their thick-walled presence, their sense of order, the way in which building and landscape belong to each other. The material substance of the Getty Complex must come out of the history and regional tradition of California, out of its colors and textures, its openness, warmth, and ease, as well as out of a timeless tradition of architecture itself. Sensitive to the natural tactilities of materials, and solidly, precisely constructed, the place will have beauty and elegance, and be a classic expression of contemporary California, a fresh and eternal building.

Just two weeks after I sent this letter the very protracted selection process suddenly came to an end. At about six-thirty p.m. on October 26, 1984, I was having dinner with my young children, Joseph, five, and Ana, three, in our apartment in New York when the telephone rang. It was Harold Williams. "I have just come out of the board meeting and we want you as the architect," he said. "It was hard, it was difficult, but I'm really happy. We made the right decision." Later that night, I received a confirmation telegram from Williams expressing his great anticipation of the pleasure of working together on this exciting project. I was elated. I had never been through a selection process like this in my life. I felt a fleeting moment of triumph. I had a glass of wine to celebrate and watched my children finish their dinner. They were too young to understand just what this meant to me or what, eventually, it would also mean to them.

It was some time before I gained any insight into the full rationale behind my selection. One factor that seems to have counted with the trustees was that, unlike Maki and Stirling, I was willing to establish a fully active presence in Los Angeles. While they liked Maki's work in Japan and Stirling's museum in Stuttgart, they also wondered whether these unique achievements could be replicated in the United States.

without the high levels of Japanese and German craftsmanship. In an interview in the fall 1985 issue of *The Harvard Architecture Review,* Williams conceded that the committee members had also been concerned about the ironic tone of Stirling's work. They seemed to have felt that his eclectic wit might not be appreciated on the West Coast of the United States.

Despite my selection, it soon became clear that the Getty directors and the trustees were determined to keep a tight hold on the design process. I knew they did not want an all-white building, but for a while I remained unsure how far I would be expected to compromise my approach. My uncertainty was reinforced by the remarks of Nancy Englander in an interview in the same issue of *The Harvard Architecture Review.* In response to the general line of questioning, she said:

> [Meier] really saw a totally different vocabulary, on this site and for this project, than the one he customarily used. . . . We had discussions about the importance of a modern expression that would harmonize with the rather traditional and universal values being dealt with by the Getty Institution. [We felt that] the building should reflect some of the philosophy of the institution but that doesn't have to translate into anything monumental that somehow makes the symbol more important than the substance. We have a very dramatic site with views out over Los Angeles. Whatever is on the site will be a visual indication of the place. . . . One of the challenges is how to provide a sense of accessibility to the museum while at the same time providing a contemplative atmosphere for the study center and conservation institute. . . . Assuming that [Meier] fulfills all requirements for function and requirements for sense of scale and character for the building, we have come out feeling that an architect has to be able to express himself as an artist-architect. There is going to be a certain rhythm and character of the spaces that is going to be Meier.

In the same interview, Williams said: "I think that the Richard Meier who comes out will be different than the one who went in, because of the whole process." Looking back, I have to ask myself whether the

Getty selection committee was under some misapprehension that I would perhaps be the most malleable of the finalists. My selection prompted huge international press attention. Like the Getty Trust, the press praised what I had done in the past, but it also speculated as to whether I would be able to respond to the challenging commission with something discernibly different.

Chapter 3   The Program Phase

I had been involved in the Getty selection process for over a year. I still did not know how long it would take to design and construct the Center, but I suspected it would be far longer than either Harold Williams or any of the trustees imagined. They were scarcely reassured when I reminded them that in earlier times cathedrals had taken generations to build. Today, even the hardiest investor is reluctant to embark on a building project knowing that completion is thirteen years away.

Twelve months after my appointment, the organizational chart of the institution finally spelled out that the J. Paul Getty Fine Arts Center would comprise the J. Paul Getty Museum, the Getty Center for the History of Art and the Humanities, the Getty Conservation Institute, the Getty Art History Information Program, and the Getty Center for Education in the Arts: five major components in all.

In my first conversation with Williams after my appointment, we speculated how long we would need for the project. At one point, he asked me if I thought it could be completed within three years. I quickly responded that I expected it would take at least ten. I explained to him that we had yet to establish the program, let alone arrive at a schematic design, obtain all the city approvals, and above all negotiate the constraints stated in the conditional use permit. I told him that we would have to develop a design to meet the needs of a very complex client body, and then to prepare all the working drawings, put these out for bid, and sign contracts before construction could begin. In brief, I thought at the time that we would need five years for the planning phase and at least five more years for construction.

Despite my experience, my estimate proved unpersuasive. The first overall work schedule presented by Karsten/Hutman Margolf, the consultants hired by the Getty in 1984, suggested that the entire project would take eight years from start to finish. They estimated that the design stage would be completed by October 1, 1988, and that the Center would be ready for occupation on October 1, 1992. As it turned out, even my original, conservative forecast was optimistic.

Before advancing any further, I had to negotiate the architectural contract with the Getty, not only to establish procedure for compensation, but also in order to define my legal, financial, and professional responsibilities. Having been through the process many times before, I imagined this would be a fairly straightforward matter. I simply sent the Getty the American Institute of Architects contract, which in its standard format provides appropriate space for such details as time frame, scope of work, fee, and other ancillary conditions. But, as I was to be often reminded, this was no ordinary project.

As Harold Williams explained to me in a letter of November 26, 1984, the Getty still had no program on which to base any kind of contract. He informed me that the selection procedure had been predicated on the assumption that the architect would participate in the development of the program and that this was something for which appropriate compensation would have to be considered in addition to the provisions of the AIA standard contract. He reminded me that this would inevitably involve a great deal of negotiation and careful planning for all of us. Since the Getty still had little idea of its program needs, he suggested that a phased contractual agreement should be used so that the extent of the work and the appropriate fee could be determined as we went along.

After a great deal of negotiation, the Getty lawyers prepared their own contract, but this still left many issues undefined. Not only were all

Two views of the Getty Center site: The top view is looking south and the bottom is north toward Santa Monica and the ocean beyond.

references to the cost of construction deftly excluded but there were also many ambiguities as to the phases of the job and my involvement in each of the stages. I held my ground, insisting that I should be hired as the architect for the duration of the project. Finally, Williams and I met for lunch at the Four Seasons restaurant in New York and resolved most of the outstanding issues, agreeing that we should eliminate any reference to a completion date. I recall Williams saying, "Whatever length of time it takes, that is the time it will take."

In the end the most unusual aspect of the final contract prepared by the Getty lawyers was that the agreement exempted me from any responsibility whatsoever for the cost of construction. Normally when the program and the budget are established in advance, the architect is required to adjust his design accordingly. In this project, the cost of work would be theirs and not mine. Nor was the allocation of expenditures for different parts of the project to be my responsibility. As it happened, this would prove to be double-edged: it enabled me to use quality materials irrespective of a fixed budget, but it also enabled the Getty to control its resources and distribute them as they saw fit.

As I previously agreed, I opened an office in Los Angeles. We eventually found a loft space on the top floor of a three-story building in Westwood, no more than a five-minute drive from the site. Five architects in my New York office immediately prepared to move to the West Coast, among them Michael Palladino, a talented young associate who would eventually play an important role in the Los Angeles office. Michael's input was seminal, from the evolution of the design to the development of the detailed construction. Trained at Virginia Polytechnic Institute and Harvard University, Palladino had already worked with me on several museums—in Frankfurt, Atlanta, and Des Moines. Although he was only thirty-three when we opened our Los Angeles office, I knew he had both the maturity and the reassuring personality that would enable us to carry the project through to a successful conclusion. Michael was totally committed to maintaining design quality and I was confident that we would make a good team. Time has proven me right.

A little later, Don Barker joined the firm as one of the senior architects involved in the project. Don had been a classmate of mine at Cornell and had a substantial practice of his own in Denver. He was a mature and experienced architect and he remained a quiet pillar of strength in the Los Angeles office throughout the job.

The Getty had made it clear that I had to remain within easy reach for consultation and even stipulated that I should spend a substantial amount of time each month in Los Angeles. At first I stayed at the Bel-Air Hotel, but after a year I moved into a single-story one-bedroom house bought earlier by the Getty on the periphery of the site, which became my California home for the duration of the entire project.

I was surprised when the Getty decided to establish a design advisory committee, a decision that suggested that I would have to deal with a considerable amount of outside advice. Williams's letter informing me of the decision already displayed a certain anxiety. It seemed to me at the time that the main rationalization for such a committee was that it would prove helpful at the program planning stage. Yet it seemed ominous that, so soon after choosing its architect, the Getty was seeking second opinions. As it turned out, my fears were unfounded. The committee was chaired by Bill Lacy and included Ada Louise Huxtable, former architecture critic of *The New York Times*; graphic designer Saul Bass; architects Frank Gehry and Ricardo Legorreta; and arts patron J. Irwin Miller. I met with them six times between 1986 and 1990, and their comments were invariably helpful. More to the point, they helped reassure the members of the board of trustees that their architectural commission was in capable hands.

I slowly realized that this was the way the Getty Trust liked to work. While it may have suggested a certain lack of confidence, one of its primary effects was to forestall criticism by outside specialists. Before acquiring a major work of art, the Getty Museum in Malibu consulted a group of outside advisers made up of curators and art historians. So, as far as the Getty was concerned, the creation of a design advisory committee was normal procedure. This was just one among the various committees of experts that are regularly constituted to advise the Getty Museum, the Conservation Institute, and the Research Institute for the History of Art and the Humanities on everything from acquisitions and program development to the hiring of senior staff.

Still, before any serious design issues could be addressed, the Getty had to define its specific programs. The museum, the only part of the institution that had been previously established, presented few difficulties with respect to its content. While it had a rich collection, an experienced staff, and, in John Walsh, a seasoned director, it had yet to define how much space would be needed to house its collection. With the Conservation Institute, the Research Institute for the History of Art and the Humanities, and the grant program, the situation was even vaguer since it was not just a question of calculating space needs. All three were new programs and were still in the process of defining themselves—their constitutions, mandates, and operating procedures. Until they had established their institutional structures, it was hard to determine what physical form they should take. To encourage dialogue on these issues, the Getty established a new building program committee made up of, in addition to Williams, Englander, and Lacy, John Walsh and Kurt Forster—the directors of the museum and the Research Institute for the History of Art and the Humanities—plus Stephen Rountree, who had been recently appointed director of the building program. Rountree had previously served the trust in various management positions, and his experience was to become relevant to his role as intermediary between ourselves and the programs that made up the institution as a whole.

The first full meeting of the building program committee, on November 30, 1984, was devoted more to scheduling questions than to discussion of the specific programs of each institution. Later, it transpired that Williams believed that the Center should be "program-driven"—that is, he was convinced that it should not be tightly run from the top down. In this sense, he thought the parts should amount to more than the whole in giving shape to the institution.

I found this to be an admirable position, but it demanded that each of the key programs create a strong identity for itself. It was obvious that the Conservation Institute had to ask itself what it intended to conserve. It had to determine where it could be most effective. The Research Institute for the History of Art and the Humanities had to decide whether it would be only a library for scholars or whether it would also initiate cultural programs of its own. Should access be restricted, or should the Research Institute be opened to a wider public?

Realizing that so many complex questions had to be resolved, I spent a good deal of time in discussion with the different program directors. One of them, Luis Monreal, an art historian of Catalan origin who had just been appointed head of the Conservation Institute, believed that fairly strong ties should be established between his department and the museum. Kurt Forster, an architectural historian of Swiss origin, had the best sense in this early period of the need for the Getty Center architecture to embody the substance of its institutional programs. Ironically, as it turned out, the Center for the History of Art, which Forster headed, was the only program substantially redesigned at a later stage because of the evolving nature of its brief. Walsh seemed to regard the architecture of the museum largely as a vessel into which he would "pour" the collection. I knew that he was anxious about the contextual relationship between classical painting and the confines of a contemporary building. This anxiety may have had its origin in his experience as a curator of painting at the Museum of Fine Arts in Boston during the period when the architect I. M. Pei was designing an extension for this building; I came to realize that Walsh had been extremely unhappy with both the process and the final result.

To help address the many questions about the programs, the building program committee and I went on a few European and American tours in 1985. We visited monuments and sites, not only to study analogous architectural and cultural institutions, but also to analyze how various museums, libraries, and cultural centers had responded to the kinds of problems we were confronting. In February, we made a joint study tour of several museums and cultural institutions in the United States. We looked at the National Gallery of Art in Washington, designed by John Russell Pope, together with its East Wing addition by I. M. Pei. While in Washington we also went to the Freer Gallery of Art, designed by Charles A. Platt, before moving on to New Haven to the Mellon Center for British Art and the Yale University Art Gallery, both designed by Louis Kahn. We then went to New York to tour the Frick Collection, the Pierpont Morgan Library, and the Metropolitan Museum of Art, the first two offering the intimacy of large houses transformed into museums, the last being an endless enfilade of rooms serving as a repository for the world of art. We ended the tour in Ohio, spending time in both the

This was one of the ridges that was kept largely intact and which formed one end of the axis crossing the site; downtown Los Angeles can be seen in the distance.
Opposite: *Grading of the eastern slope of the complex transformed the hillside.*

53

Cleveland Museum of Art and the Toledo Museum of Art. Kurt Forster indicated that none of the buildings we visited came close to solving all the multifarious problems that confronted the Getty Center, although he felt we had learned something. Understandably enough, John Walsh was critical of the lighting conditions in most of the galleries we visited, and he reminded us that the museums we had seen were not to be taken as models but rather as buildings that exemplified successful and unsuccessful solutions to an equal degree. Like other members of the tour, I was particularly aware of negative examples, such as the American wing of the Metropolitan Museum, where the freestanding partitions impose a uniform hanging height, and the overexposure of delicate manuscripts in the brightly lit corridors of the Pierpont Morgan Library. I also noticed several depressing features they had in common, such as the more or less conventional way in which art was exhibited, and the largely uninspired character of the galleries themselves. This generated a great deal of discussion about what we ought to avoid.

In late May and early June of that same year, we flew to Munich to visit three extraordinary museums, each representing a building from a different period of history—the eighteenth, nineteenth, and twentieth centuries. These were the Glyptothek, the Alte Pinakothek, and the Neue Pinakothek. We then went on to Verona to look at the part fourteenth-century, part Napoleonic Museo Castelvecchio, which had been beautifully refurbished by the Italian architect Carlo Scarpa in the late 1950s. From there, we drove to Florence, touring the nearby Certosa del Galluzzo to study, as Le Corbusier had, the monastery's organization around courtyards and the relationship between interior and exterior spaces. Finally, we visited the Villa d'Este in Tivoli, the Villa Lante in Bagnaia, and the Palazzo Farnese in Caprarola to examine their spectacular gardens, paying particular attention, with our own landscape in mind, to the deployment of pools and fountains as spaces within the garden form. This trip was extremely fruitful since it enabled us to talk openly and informally about ideas related to the Getty Center.

Although the design process was still on hold, there was much to do. I was responsible for coordinating engineering and technical consultants and was soon involved with many of them in a host of preliminary studies, such as an extensive investigation of the soil quality on the site and the likely response of the site's geology to seismic movement. We also studied the incidence of soil erosion and what steps we might take to control it. We began planning a large underground parking structure at the entry to the site, alongside the San Diego Freeway; that was the first structure to be built.

A more immediate problem was posed by the many concerns being expressed by the Brentwood Homeowners' Association, which represented the prosperous residents of the neighborhood south and west of the Getty site. Later, this same association would besiege us, but in 1985 and 1986 we were still confident of allaying its anxieties about the size, location, and color of the new Center. Brentwood was the only residential neighborhood worried about the new Getty. The residents of Bel Air wholeheartedly supported the project from the beginning. In February 1985, I responded in what I thought was a reassuring manner to a letter from Hugh Snow, one of the lawyers for the Brentwood association. I told him that what we had in mind was a horizontal structure, sensitive to the natural landscape and respectful of human scale.

Stephen Rountree, as director of the Getty building program, assumed responsibility for all community relations; he met frequently with the association's representatives throughout the project. On February 13, 1986, I made my first cautious appearance before the group at the invitation of its president, Mario Piatelli. Fortunately, I had told Piatelli in advance that I would not be bringing plans or drawings with me for purposes of review. Yet when he introduced me to what was effectively a town meeting, he noted with some disappointment that I would be merely explaining my general approach. A transcript of my remarks and the question-and-answer session that followed confirmed the relatively convivial nature of our initial exchange. It also revealed how the situation rather quickly turned sour.

I began by stressing that I was fully cognizant of the association's concerns, all of which I believed would be addressed while the complex was being designed over the next two years. At that moment, I explained, we were studying how to organize the buildings on the site while responding to the natural topography and the unique character of the light. I informed them that we would enrich the landscape with additional greenery, creating parklike settings, with internal courtyards as well as places to sit and walk. I emphasized the fact that the result would not be a typical institutional building but rather a complex of interrelated buildings in which human scale would remain a paramount consideration throughout.

I felt I could not avoid addressing the issue of the color and tone of the external finishes, even though I could think of little to say that might totally reassure the association. I argued that the color of the site itself would have some bearing on the choice of materials and the relationship between various kinds of cladding, including stone. I went on to say that it was too early to be specific and I added that I hoped to be able to show them a detailed design in a year's time. I then invited questions.

The audience was evidently not won over. The first questioner wondered how I could meet the association's demands if the Getty decided that it wanted to build a monument on the hill. I reassured them that the Getty did not aspire to create a monumental institution and, since I knew this to be the case, I had no hesitation in making the point. The next questioner asserted that my work involved "vast, shiny, white steel and marble walls, while we see our hills as something soft, gentle, golden in tone, and earth-colored and we wish to preserve them like that." I responded that every building that I had been involved with had been designed in relation to its surroundings, which in this case would mean reacting to the color, texture, and topography of the site and therefore would favor the use of a natural material.

The association's third concern, namely the sight lines, took up the rest of the discussion. To put it bluntly, the Brentwood residents did not want to see—or be seen from—the Getty Center. One homeowner mentioned the neighborhood's security problems and expressed fear that "people" visiting the Getty could use the site "for making an observation of the nearby homes," which was also the gist of remarks by another somewhat agitated member of the audience: "We have been informed by the Getty Trust that according to the lines of sight . . . residences lying to the west of the property will not be seen. But in your remarks this evening you made mention of the beauty of the view of the Pacific from the site. Are you prepared to sacrifice that beauty by keeping the buildings below the brow of the hill?"

I countered by explaining that it would not be possible to view the ocean from the site without the buildings being visible from the surrounding areas. On the other hand, I added that the nature of the topography was such that some of the homeowners would not really see the building at all, although I conceded that parts of the complex would always be visible from Sunset Boulevard. As for security concerns, I tried to assure them that every effort would be made not to create major public spaces on the south promontory ridge. I followed up by pointing out that since strong southern sun was the enemy of art, the museum would certainly not have windows facing south. With that, the meeting ended and Mr. Piatelli invited the audience to give me a big hand. The applause was modest, to say the least.

As things turned out, this meeting was nothing but an overture. Over the next six years, it was almost impossible to appease the constantly escalating demands of the homeowners' association, which came to adopt the infamous stance known as NIMBY, or "Not in my backyard." The association's attitude, it seemed to me, was "We're happy you're there, but we don't want to see you, we don't want to hear you, and we don't want to smell you." The association was skilled at using the local press, and many of its members had sufficient political influence to delay the necessary approvals by the Los Angeles Planning Commission. Through such tactics, further concessions were readily extracted from the Getty.

Some of these had a major impact on the design and method of construction. Negotiations over the maximum permitted height of the Center dragged on for months. Rountree, who showed astonishing patience in dealing with the homeowners, would call and say: "I think we can get thirty-five feet. Is that enough?" I would then make a rapid reassessment on the spot and invariably answer something like "No, we can't do it in thirty-five feet. In fact, we need at least forty-five feet." For the two-story museum complex, for example, we initially requested a height limit of eighty feet but eventually settled for a maximum height limit of sixty-five feet. But the next issue in dispute was the exact point from which the sixty-five feet would be measured. We finally agreed that the ground level should coincide with the threshold of the museum. By this time, I had spent many months wandering over the

The shaping of the site took a great deal of time, since aside from making permanent access roads, a huge amount of terrain had to be cut away, relocated, and stabilized.

site and I was thoroughly familiar with its constantly varying topography. I knew fairly well what could or could not be seen from each different vantage point. With this knowledge in hand, I recommended that the threshold of the museum be established at 916 feet above sea level. Even then, we were eventually forced to reduce this by a further twenty feet, finalizing the level at 896 feet above sea level. This compromise ultimately derived from the specious reasoning of the Getty lawyers, who insisted that nine hundred feet was not a good number.

Soon after this concession, we found ourselves in yet another bind when the homeowners demanded that the Center be built without removing any earth from the site because they did not want to be disturbed by endless convoys of trucks carrying soil from the hill. Ironically, while they insisted that the volume of the site not be reduced, we had to excavate in order to satisfy their other demand for reducing the height of the building. In the end, throughout the design process, we were constantly calculating how much earth would be displaced by the buildings and their foundations. And we had no choice but to find a place for the excavated earth on the site, a juggling operation that continually altered the landscape. It also cost a great deal to transport the earth, install the foundations and the undercroft, backfill the earth, and then regrade the adjacent topography for each and every structure. It proved to be an unbelievably onerous concession made to the homeowners well before any real work had been carried out on the site.

In March 1986, I was given the definitive architectural program, in which the various component parts of the Getty Center were sufficiently defined to begin the design. I had, of course, been thinking about the design all along, but now the program needs were defined in some detail. Employing rough volumetric models to represent each of the institutions, we began to develop the concept of a cultural campus, the form of which responded to the topography of the site and was aligned to existing axes found in the Los Angeles grid. The site would be entered from Sepulveda Boulevard through an existing tunnel under the San Diego Freeway. The parking area was logically situated adjacent to this entry, and from here a road wound its way up the hillside to the main campus level. This coincided with the entry of the museum, which was the principal public destination.

The site was made up of two ridges running roughly north-south: one, the eastern ridge, being virtually parallel to the San Diego Freeway as it runs past the site; the other, the western ridge, seeming to correspond to the angle of the same freeway as it leaves the grid of the city going north through Sepulveda Pass. As is apparent from one of my earliest sketches, I imagined the complex as a long museum spine running along the eastern ridge, taking off from the crest of the access road as it entered the campus. In this sketch, dated September 4, 1986, the museum complex extended along the eastern ridge to culminate on a promontory facing south over the city, while the rest of the museum looked laterally out over the freeway, Century City, and the UCLA campus. Already, the Center's private side, the contemplative spaces for the scholars working at the Research Institute for the History of Art and the Humanities, was situated at the extreme limit of the western ridge, looking out over Brentwood toward the Pacific. The administration building was placed on the other promontory, at the northern end of the eastern ridge, the balancing polar opposite, as it were, of the Research Institute for the History of Art and the Humanities. But ideas at this stage were still embryonic, although clearly influenced by the existing topography.

I had, of course, yet to design any of the buildings themselves, but the Center's basic form as seen from the air was becoming apparent. Indeed, as I look back at the early sketches and models, the linear process and the relationship of the buildings to each other and to the landform have held up through all the subsequent changes.

In September 1986, I presented the first preliminary design for the whole site to the design advisory committee. Our large plaster model showed both the topography of the site and the initial massing of the buildings. This presentation did not elicit too much discussion since a large part of the meeting was devoted to visiting the site.

What followed was more trying: we entered a seemingly endless series of meetings with various committees, including the building program committee headed by Stephen Rountree, who was responsible for negotiating with the homeowners' association and the Los Angeles City Council. Time after time, we discussed the location of the access roads leading from the main entry to the top of the hill, the general massing of the buildings, and the percentage of space required above- and below-ground in order to satisfy the stringent requirements established by the sight lines set forth in the conditional use permit.

At this time, we were engaged in a great deal of strategic planning. We had not only to address such concerns as the location of stoplights on Sepulveda Boulevard, but also to develop a strategy for maintaining the land itself. Since the slopes were being regraded and much of the native chaparral brush had been removed from the site in order to reduce fire risk, we had to devise ways of stabilizing the ground to prevent soil erosion. A further problem arose from the astonishing amount of wildlife on site, mostly coyotes and snakes. The latter constituted a serious problem during the clearing of the chaparral. The landscape workers were provided with a snake chart so that they would be able to identify which species were dangerous; they were all armed with machetes in order to dispose of these. My children, too, were soon made aware of the wildlife when they came to stay with me on the site. As they walked up the path to the house they were greeted by a huge rattler curled up on the front doorstep and ready to strike. A man with a machete had to be sent for.

One never-ending debate was how the general public would gain access to the top of the hill and, moreover, what sort of open space, pedestrian walkways, and general amenities should be provided once they reached the Getty campus. This led us into arcane discussions about noise, not only noise emanating from outside the site, such as the freeway, but also the noise that might be generated by the Center itself, by the general public, and particularly by any mechanical systems for carrying visitors to the crest of the hill. And just to make such discussions more frustratingly confusing, the final size of the project had yet to be established. In fact, both the size and the configuration of the project were ultimately determined through a kind of negative procedure because the conditional use permit, as finally granted on March 11, 1985, more or less defined what we could not do: we could not build beyond a certain height or specified area; we could not work outside set hours; we could not be seen from certain locations, and so on. It was clear that the Brentwood Homeowners' Association wielded considerable influence.

One key issue under discussion since 1985 was how many visitors could be expected to come to the Getty on both peak weekends and

The size and operation of these enormous machines fascinated me; my daughter, Ana (bottom), *shows the huge scale of the graders.*

weekdays. These estimates would define the on-site parking needs, not only for visitors but also for the staff members. It was evident that it would not be possible to accommodate much parking at the top of the hill, but early soil tests determined that a large underground parking structure at the point of entry was feasible. All that remained were two imponderables: first, how much parking should be provided for visitors and employees respectively; and second, how the visitor would travel from the main parking garage to the complex at the top.

Initial estimates established the required parking accommodation for visitors at a maximum of a thousand cars, to be stacked underground on four or five levels, but this provision was revised upward early in July 1986 to sixteen hundred cars on six subterranean levels for visitors and 750 cars in underground parking at the top of the hill for nine hundred employees. This parking requirement was based on revised attendance projections, then standing at an average of six thousand people daily or approximately 1.3 million visitors a year.

Once this had been determined we entered into protracted discussion as to the best means of transporting visitors from the base to the crest of the hill. A whole range of options—buses and travelators; funicular systems; various modes of fixed-rail traction—were discussed, but finally a noiseless form of electrical tram riding on an air-cushion rail was chosen to shuttle between the parking at the base of the hill and the arrival plaza of the campus at the top.

A second meeting of the design advisory committee took place on December 10, 1986, when I presented the first of many wooden models of the project. Each presentation was accompanied by fairly detailed drawings showing the planning of each building plus its initial connections and the relationship between the interior spaces and the landscape. The committee members could easily see that there had been changes since our last meeting. This caused a certain amount of contradictory comment. Some members preferred the earlier version, in which the gallery clusters of the museum were more closely integrated with the landscape, while others thought that the museum was all the better for becoming more self-contained. At one moment, Ada Louise Huxtable raised my spirits by urging me not to pay too much heed to criticism from the Getty staff; this advice conveniently overlooked the fact that the staff in question formed part of the very same advisory committee. Huxtable was also concerned that the then hermetic character of the museum would be allowed to become unduly monumental. Ricardo Legorreta, the distinguished Mexican architect, argued that the general circulation ought to follow the looser pattern of movement that I had adopted in the Frankfurt museum. Such advice is easily given and often extremely difficult to act upon.

Meanwhile, Harold Williams was growing increasingly alarmed over the escalating estimates of the cost of construction, and with good reason. When the project had been first revealed to the public the Getty was still uncertain as to the program, and the trust was able to announce a projected cost of somewhere in the region of $100 million. In the fall of 1986, two years after I had been appointed, Williams and Rountree were advised by Karsten/Hutman Margolf that the estimated construction cost of the Getty Center would probably be more like $300 million. Just six months later, in April 1987, in order to create a more effective construction process, the Getty appointed Dinwiddie Construction Company as construction manager. Dinwiddie soon came up with the alarming news that their estimated budget was now at around $500 million. As a result Williams and his advisers kept pressing for cost-cutting measures. However, no matter how many reductions were introduced, nothing seemed able to stop the estimated cost from growing—and we still had not begun construction. Astonishingly, by the fall of 1988, the Getty's own cost analysts—that is to say, the combined wisdom of Dinwiddie Construction Company and Karsten/Hutman Margolf—indicated that the construction budget was now approaching $680 million.

One of the main difficulties, aside from those posed by the escalating costs, involved determining what could be built within the permitted three-dimensional site profile. The Brentwood Homeowners' Association continued to campaign against the Getty Center, going so far as to issue warnings that the Getty was engaged in flagrant violations of the conditional use permit. They implied that we were planning to build to a height of 120 feet and to double the allowable occupied area of building. And while these charges were baseless, they served to agitate the community still further. A "Committee to Save

The earthmoving equipment was parked and lined up on a level part of the site at the end of each working day. The physical demands on the machinery meant that there had to be an on-site repair yard with many spare parts.

West L.A." appeared in the late spring of 1987, claiming that twelve thousand additional cars would soon be occupying the San Diego Freeway every weekend and demanding that the city order a fresh environmental impact report.

There was method to this madness, particularly since the city planning commission was scheduled to begin hearings on the schematic design in May 1987 with, we hoped, the intent of approving the Center's master plan by late June. Playing its cards well at the hearings, the homeowners' association won a host of fresh concessions from the Getty. Finally, on June 24, 1987, the belligerent neighbors signed an agreement with the Getty that defined the 107 points of the conditional use permit. The previously negotiated height restrictions were formally incorporated into the permit, but in addition the Getty had to agree that all exteriors "will be clad principally with natural stone." The agreement stated that "a spectrum of colors and surface textures" would be allowed, but that "white stone will not be used." It also stipulated that "no white porcelain panels or mirrored glass" should be used on the perimeter elevations facing the community.

This agreement, which as far as I knew was unprecedented in its scope, went on to include limitations covering sight lines into Brentwood and a pledge by the Getty to restrict the use of artificial light at night so as not to disturb the neighboring properties. It was further agreed that the built area of the Getty Center would not exceed 505,000 square feet of space that could be occupied. In the end, the total constructed area would amount to the 900,000 square feet that had been previously agreed upon. Needless to say, much of this space, including parking, storage areas, book stacks, and electrical and mechanical services, had to be located underground. Further restrictions were imposed on noise, and a portion of the Getty complex had to be partially hidden from Sunset Boulevard by a screen of tall evergreens. The association also won thirty days in which it could review the final construction drawings before they were formally submitted to the California Department of Building and Safety for approval and issuance of the building permit.

The master plan was finally approved by the Los Angeles Planning Commission on June 25, 1987. At a public hearing our plans for the

Getty were fully endorsed by the councilmen, the commissioners, and various community leaders. Our elation at this decision, however, was tempered by the knowledge that our long struggle with the homeowners' association was by no means over. Ten years later, the association would still be making demands on the Getty. A few days after receiving the city's approval, I warned Rountree that we could expect new delays when our construction documents were complete and we were ready to go into construction. It was painfully clear to me that we still had a long way to go.

Nevertheless, the city's approval of the conditional use permit meant there was no turning back and that we now knew the ground rules under which we would have to work. These covered landscape treatment, traffic provisions, parking limits, cross-sectional profiles, setbacks, sight lines, the general range of permitted external finishes, and the overall size and height of the buildings, plus grade level at the point of entry and limitations on the ultimate size of the basement. It was also triumphantly reported in the local press that the permit specifically excluded the use of white stone and assured for some that their residences would be shielded from the prying eyes of visitors to the Center.

By now I was well prepared for the long haul. The staff in my Los Angeles office was growing rapidly. We had fifty architects working on the project and within a short time the number rose to nearly one hundred. We created our own model shop near the Westwood office; I have a feeling that this may have been one of the most effective model shops ever set up by an architectural practice. We had about five thousand square feet of light-industrial space with some upstairs storage rooms; the main skylit work space measured thirty-two by seventy-five feet and was equipped with large garage-type doors. This opening was enlarged in 1991 to handle the tall models of the museum galleries we made in the shop. We moved into the space in April 1987 and built up the machinery and workshop from scratch. In the most intense period we had eleven people working in the model shop for several months, mostly on the two large site models we built to eighth-inch and quarter-inch scale. This entire operation was brilliantly run for us by a young Californian named Michael Gruber, who aside from being an architect was also an exquisite craftsman. The workshop built models more or

The five-thousand-square-foot model shop was in a light-industrial space where, starting in 1987, eleven staff members worked continuously on the two hundred study models and six large gallery models built to quarter-inch scale. Nearly every aspect of the complex was studied in model form, which was particularly useful in conveying the design.

The model of site study 1, which was
the first preliminary scheme of September 1986: the museum galleries
are around a patio, the Research
Institute is housed in a cube, and the
arroyo is treated as a stepped terrace
garden. The close correspondence
between the podium configuration
and the contours of the site is clearly
defined.

This area around the arroyo was radi-
cally reshaped; here one sees the steep-
ness of the grade and a few carefully
preserved trees.
Opposite: *Since no earth could be
removed from the site, it was necessary
to stockpile the displaced soil in
mounds before redepositing it elsewhere.*

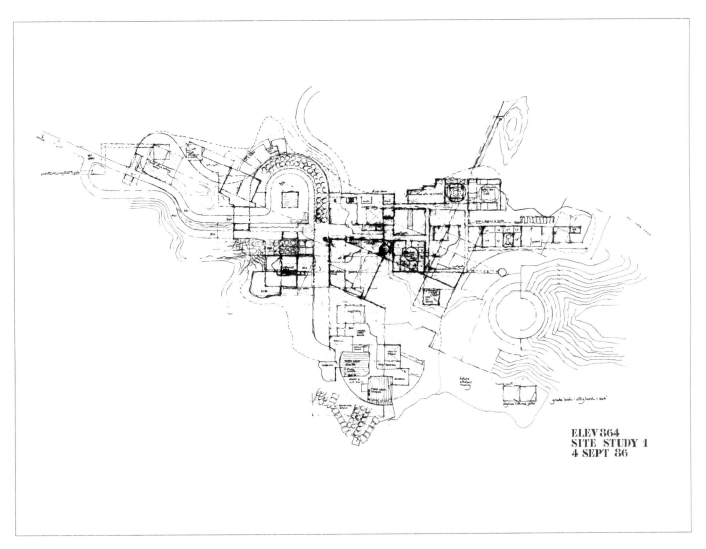

ELEV 864
SITE STUDY 1
4 SEPT 86

These September 1986 sketches reveal
two alternatives prior to the preparation of drawings for the first
schematic-design presentation.
Above: *Access to the site was by
automobile with a horseshoe-shaped
drop-off area in front of the museum.*
Opposite: *The idea of an electrical
tramway access is being examined
with a corresponding change in the
road layout.*

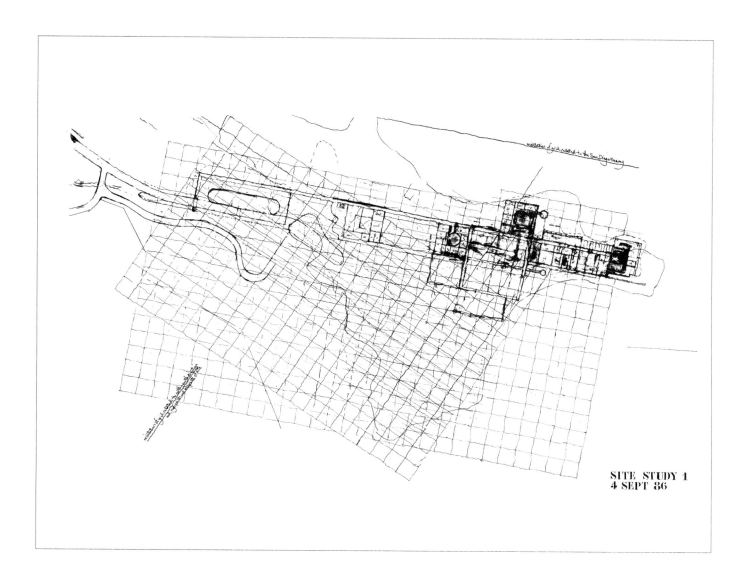

oscillation of grid related to the San Diego Freeway

oscillation of grid related to the existing beach road

SITE STUDY 1
4 SEPT 86

Top: *Kate, Ana, and Joseph walking on the site soon after I moved into my new Los Angeles home*
Bottom: *The back of the house with Ana by the swimming pool, which went under a wall into the bedroom*

less continuously at many different scales, ranging from sixteenth-inch-scale site-study models to one-inch-scale volumetric studies and three-inch-scale lighting gallery studies, which were big enough to walk in. All the models were of wood, with the exception of one plaster site model we built early on in order to represent the earth color. In all, six large models and about two hundred other study models were built. They proved critical in conveying the design to the advisory committee, Getty staff, and general public.

I also began to feel more at home in Los Angeles after moving into a house bordering the western edge of the site in 1987. The Getty had acquired the house from the previous owner, who was understandably distraught at the prospect of having a construction site in his back garden. It was a strange dwelling: a crested timber structure, slightly Oriental in feeling, with low, pitched roofs, a labyrinthine entry, a carport, and a separate guest house. In the garden, there were lemon, orange, and plum trees, which supplied us with delicious, sweet fruit. The living room and terrace had a splendid view over West Los Angeles and out toward the Pacific, while a narrow swimming pool passed below a large stone wall right into the main bedroom. When I inherited it, it was rather gloomy, dark, and rat-infested, something out of a Raymond Chandler novel. I painted the walls—white, of course—and, after what seemed an efficient extermination of the rodent population, it was inhabitable.

However, one night, after I had been living in the house for a number of years, I was awoken from a deep sleep by the strange sound of rats gnawing away at the insulation within the walls, right next to my pillow. It was nothing that a good rap on the wall would not silence, except that after sufficient time had passed for me to fall asleep again, they returned to their unseen mastications with renewed ferocity. It was the perfect recipe for a sleepless night, but happily, after a few days, the rats seemed to have sated their appetite for that particular part of the inner fabric; thereafter, they left me in peace.

The other oddity was a homeless person, whom I never met, but who was in the habit of sleeping in my bed while I was in New York. Exactly how many times he did this, we shall never know. His mode of entry was ingenious, and demonstrated a certain athletic prowess. It seems that he scaled the security fences enclosing both the site and the house and then, having gained access to the garden court and the swimming pool, he entered my bedroom by taking his clothes off and swimming under the stone wall that divided the interior of the bedroom from the exterior of the pool. He emerged virtually naked on the other side and went promptly to sleep in my bed. There he was discovered recumbent on two separate occasions by the night watchman. On the first occasion, he was dressed down by the watchman and sent packing with his clothes; on the second, however, he was taken down to the police station and stuck in jail for the night—which seems to have cured him of the habit. Since these events took place in my absence, they didn't really disturb me, except that I felt a little uneasy at the prospect that he might appear one night, only to discover that what he had assumed to be an unoccupied bed was, in fact, filled with my sleeping form. His antennae were good, however; this somewhat alarming scenario never occurred. The house became a kind of permanent residence where work and pleasure could be readily combined and where I could openly and easily receive friends and visitors as I began to settle into my constant commuting between New York and California. It was a relief not to have to live in a hotel; having the house enabled my children to be with me during their vacations, and in my home away from home they were able to enjoy the view, the fruit trees, the pool, and the sun. I always seemed to be receiving visitors in a somewhat ad hoc way, since my exotic abode and the spectacular site were a curious combination not to be passed up too easily. My friends as well as colleagues from the Getty would pay me the occasional visit to see how I was getting on in my isolation.

I loved living close to the site, and for three years before construction began, it was like having my own park. At weekends and on late summer evenings when I was alone, I would wander over the hilltop, taking in the view, but also trying to picture how different versions of the basic concept would work in practice. Soon enough, I knew, I would have to make up my mind, once and for all.

Chapter 4   The Design Takes Shape

Evolution of the design was slow because so many issues remained undecided, including the overall philosophy and mandate of the institution and the specific space needs of the different programs. In addition, we had still to appoint the various technical consultants who are essential to a commission of this scale, from the structural, mechanical, and electrical engineers to the lighting, acoustical, security, audiovisual, and laboratory consultants, and to what was, in this case, the all too crucial choice of the landscape architect.

The search for a landscape architect had gone on for over a year. We needed someone who could not only expand on the work of the geotechnical, soil, civil, and traffic engineering consultants, but also had the capacity to advise on the installation of new vegetation and the consolidation and maintenance of the landscape. This person should have experience of southern California and therefore understand the local climate and its impact on the character of the landscape. The ideal candidate should also be familiar with the local seismic and drainage conditions and know how to deal with the wildlife. Together with John Walsh and Stephen Rountree, we reviewed the work of at least a dozen landscape architects of many nationalities, finally settling on Emmet Wemple, who had been the landscape architect for the Getty Museum in Malibu.

The Getty was prepared to leave the selection of the structural, mechanical, and electrical consultants to me, reviewing and ratifying my recommendations. I chose Robert Englekirk as the main structural engineer because of his particular expertise in southern California anti-seismic construction, while John Altieri and his partner, Ken Weiber, were selected as the mechanical, electrical, and plumbing consultants because I had worked with them before and because they had been involved in the refurbishment and expansion of the Metropolitan Museum of Art in New York. As might have been foreseen in a project of such complexity and duration, two of the major consultants, Wemple and Altieri, who were both of advanced age, decided to retire shortly after the schematic-design phase was completed, causing a hiatus in what would otherwise have been a continuously evolving process. Luckily, Ken Weiber had been intimately involved from the beginning, and he and his associates were able to continue the mechanical work. The saga of the landscape architect proved much more complex.

In preparing the detailed design of the Getty Center, my first priority was the museum complex, not only because it was the most public entity, but also because the museum's program was the first to be completed. We had already decided that the Getty Center should not be a single monolithic structure, but rather several buildings that would emphasize the semi-autonomous status of the various institutes. This approach was echoed by the decision to divide the museum into a series of pavilion clusters, thereby giving a separate identity to different parts of the collection.

With this approach, it became all the more important to establish an identifiable route through the museum. We began by following a format that had already been defined by John Walsh in the program: to create a generous reception area that, besides accommodating an information counter, cloakroom, and bookstore, would help to orient the visitors toward different parts of the collection. The entrance lobby to the Getty Museum was conceived as a large top-lit circular foyer. From here, visitors would look out onto the museum courtyard, flanked to the east and south by pavilions housing the permanent collection and partially enclosed on the west by a temporary-exhibition space raised above an outdoor café, overlooking the central garden. This courtyard, enclosed by the museum pavilions and enriched by fountains, plantings, and sitting areas, was intended to affirm the California character of the site.

As we refined this concept, the museum courtyard evolved into a general promenade area, which, while affording magnificent views over the surrounding landscape, also serves as a space for such outdoor events as the occasional concert. This courtyard provides a space for people to enter and leave the gallery sequence at will. And in case of inclement weather, it is possible to pass from pavilion to pavilion on both floors, via either internal corridors or covered passageways. Each pavilion cluster has its own atrium with an adjacent stairway and elevator linking the sculpture, drawing, manuscript, and photography galleries on the first floor to the painting galleries above. Throughout the museum, we maintained a layering in section between paintings, illuminated by skylights on the top floor, and artworks such as drawings and manuscripts, which must be shielded from ultraviolet light, on the lower levels.

The first pavilion cluster houses art from the medieval period to the end of the sixteenth century, while the second, third, and fourth pavilion clusters are devoted to works of art mainly from the seventeenth, eighteenth, and nineteenth centuries respectively. French decorative art, drawn largely from the eighteenth century and early nineteenth century, occupies the ground floor of the second and third pavilion clusters, while twentieth-century photography is located on the ground floor of the fourth cluster. Given this variable structure, visitors can elect to follow their own tours, taking in an entire chronological sequence or visiting only the painting galleries or simply heading straight to a favorite artwork or period.

The next priority was to design a coherent sequence of approach that traced a path from the garage to the lower tram station, the tram journey itself, and culminated in the entry plaza of the campus. On descending from the tram, the visitor would be placed approximately at the intersection between the museum axis, running parallel to the freeway below, and the garden axis, shifted twenty-two and a half degrees off this line and running diagonally through the site as the spine of the central garden. In the schematic design approved by the trustees in September

Two views of the site in June 1992. By this time the earthmoving was considerably advanced and the plan-profile of the earthworks plus the excavated area began to reflect the final placement of the buildings.

1988, the central garden axis became a promenade that ended in a loggia wall cutting across it at ninety degrees. From there, visitors could look down onto a semicircular orange grove with a reflecting pool and also beyond across the panorama of Los Angeles toward Catalina Island. My idea—and unfortunately in the end it was only an idea—was to use the lead-up to this belvedere to give the entire Center a civic-landscape character in the Italian garden tradition. What I had in mind was the scale and descending axial order of the gardens of Villa Lante in Bagnaia, Villa Garzoni in Collodi, or even, on a diminutive scale, of the American Academy in Rome. In these gardens, the landscape is defined in relation to the architecture, in contrast to the English picturesque tradition, where land and building are more autonomous.

Through a succession of designs, we attempted to strike a balance between the garden promenade and the main approach to the museum. We were conscious that the weighting of this emphasis in one direction or the other would necessarily have implications for how the Center would be perceived. The idea of the central garden as a public meditation and promenade space was integral to our initial conception of the entire complex. This space was intended to serve as a natural divide between the world of art, as represented by the museum, and the world of intellectual reflection and critical inquiry, as represented by the Research Institute for the History of Art and the Humanities. Initially we proposed that, from the entry plaza, a radial staircase would extend somewhat off-axis toward the museum entrance, while a ramp would feed more directly into the garden promenade. Later this design was further developed to include a broad flight of stairs leading directly to the museum threshold. However, this would change further as the Getty developed its own ideas for the central garden.

The painstaking process of negotiation and debate that preceded approval of the schematic design can be gauged by the fact that from 1986 on, our workshop produced nine large wooden models of varying size. The smallest was approximately four feet square while the largest was nine feet wide by twenty-eight feet long and showed the complex and the entire site. Each model embodied another state in the design development; together they led eventually to the conditional use permit model of 1987 and a remarkably precise one-sixteenth-inch-scale cherrywood model, which in its various stages took twelve people nine months to construct, and which was the focus of the presentation of the schematic design to the Getty board of trustees in September 1988.

This meeting took place at nine o'clock on a bright sunny morning in my Los Angeles office, where we had set up the model together with a large number of detailed drawings. At that time, the board was made up of the following people: Harold E. Berg, Norris Bramlett, Kenneth N. Dayton, Robert F. Erburu, John T. Fey, Gordon P. Getty, Vartan Gregorian, Jon B. Lovelace, Herbert L. Lucas, Jr., Franklin D. Murphy, Stuart T. Peeler, Rocco C. Siciliano, Jennifer Jones Simon, J. Patrick Whaley, Harold Williams, and Otto Wittmann. Although they had seen some of the conceptual models, they had never set eyes on anything as detailed as this. Yet, as they entered the room, they barely seemed to notice the model. As I began explaining the design and the ideas behind it, I felt that despite my enthusiasm and conviction the group was not yet fully focused on the project. I was beginning to grow nervous when, about fifteen minutes into my presentation, the door swung open and in walked Gordon Getty, who had just flown down from San Francisco. He took one look at the model and exclaimed: "Is that it? That's fantastic! Let's build it!" Suddenly, the mood of the meeting changed. Like most board members, Getty was only involved in the project from time to time, coming to meetings of the whole board when new phases of the project were about to begin or when the construction budget was discussed. But this was one of J. Paul Getty's sons speaking, and clearly the prestige of the name was charismatic. Thus although his vote carried no more weight than any other board member's, his spontaneous exuberance proved contagious. Other trustees were soon offering their congratulations, and the board approved the schematic design without hesitation. I was delighted, for, even if we had far to go, this vote of confidence boosted our morale enormously.

And yet this ebullient mood was fairly short-lived because, even with the board's approval of the schematic design, the situation remained strangely fluid. Various Getty programs constantly lobbied to satisfy their growing space needs, seemingly indifferent to the limitations that had been imposed upon us by the conditional use permit. And, despite constantly revised estimates of the total construction cost, we were still

The schematic-design model of
January 1988 shows (above) a view
from the north of the tram route
entering the site while (opposite)
a view from the south shows the
central garden arranged as an
amphitheater around a reflecting
pool, with a series of stepped par-
terres rising to the top of the complex site.

unable to arrive at a final figure. Steve Rountree wrote to Donald Dreusike of Dinwiddie Construction Company on October 10, 1988, to express the Getty's growing frustration and demand that the contractor verify and explain their latest cost surge.

Every time the estimated budget rose significantly, Harold Williams informed the board and sought its approval. And he naturally disliked having to do so. Before each presentation he would ask Rountree and me to suggest new ways to cut costs. This was a bewildering exercise, because we were talking in the abstract about spending or saving money on a project that was still years away from being built. And while we continued to modify the design in order to incorporate less expensive materials and details, the total cost of the proposed Center nonetheless kept on growing. This was due in part to inflation, and in part to the inability of both contractor and cost consultants to grasp the full scope of the scheme in all its technical and topographical detail.

One of the oddest budget decisions occurred shortly before we presented the schematic design to the board of trustees. With construction due to start on the North Entry parking building in 1989, and with the Getty still operating on the assumption that the entire complex would cost no more than $430 million, Dinwiddie Construction Company suddenly produced an estimate of around $680 million. Understandably, we were all shocked. Under no circumstances would Harold Williams ask the board to approve a budget above $600 million; the challenge was to reconcile two figures $80 million apart. I suggested eliminating a building and was promptly told that they wanted to build everything. I responded that there was little we could cut from the design that would make a significant impact on the overall costs. Even if we had eliminated all of the stone and drastically reduced the quality of the internal finishes, the final cost would still have far exceeded Williams's $600 million upper limit. Despite my characterization of this impasse, the Getty continued to insist that I find additional savings.

Slowly I concluded that I had no choice but to apply the most primitive logic: if the cost was 12 percent over target, we would simply have to shrink the Center by the same amount. It would be like putting a drawing into a photocopying machine and reducing it by 12 percent. In

Two views of the site in 1992: The top shows the museum ridge in June, while the bottom shows the main access road ascending the hill. The line of sandbags and the plastic covering prevented soil erosion in the winter months.

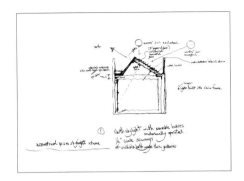

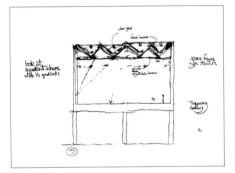

A number of options were studied for museum gallery lighting and sun control. These sketches illustrate two of the possible options for skylight louvers.
Opposite: *A study model of the loan- and special-exhibits gallery shown with horizontal roof louvers*

practice, of course, it was not so simple, because the overall reduction meant extensive redesigning and redrawing. It was a horrendous task: when the geometrical grid of the entire building changed, everything had to be adjusted accordingly. The exercise was further complicated by the fact that the height of the buildings, so painfully negotiated with the Brentwood homeowners, had to remain unchanged. Even the relationship of the buildings to each other could not be significantly altered. Nonetheless each building had to be reduced in size, although the amount of reduction varied from one building to the next. The auditorium, for instance, went from 600 to 450 seats. This enabled Williams to present the trustees with the revised target figure of $600 million in September 1988. Of course, the savings were more theoretical than real, since the need to redesign the Center brought new delays, which in turn added costs. So although we shrank the buildings by 12 percent, we did not achieve a 12 percent savings, and, within a short time, Williams had once again to discuss with the trustees the need for additional funds.

When I met the design advisory committee in January 1990, I had much to report. Using the revised schematic-design model, in which the 12 percent reduction had been incorporated, I was able to describe in detail the visitor's experience of arriving at the Getty Center by tram, first seeing the hilltop from afar, then losing sight of it, and finally seeing the complex right in front of him or her as the tram reached the entry plaza. Thus the vista from the ascending tram would naturally oscillate between the serpentine retaining wall above and the changing prospect out over the foothills of the site to the city below.

After discussing the organization and character of the buildings, we took the design advisory committee to our model shop to look at the three-quarter-sized models of the prototypical gallery spaces, which we had just completed. These models were so large that two or three people could readily sit inside them. I encouraged committee members to do exactly that so as to experience the design of the skylight and the relationship of the natural light to the space. "Everyone should see this," exclaimed Ada Louise Huxtable. "It's marvelous." Later we visited the site itself, where workers were clearing chaparral in preparation for the grading to begin later in the year. I took the committee members around the entire site, indicating the place where each building would eventually stand, although it was clear that many of the committee found it incredibly difficult to imagine what the buildings would actually look like. After this auspicious visit, we began showing these models to various members of the Getty staff together with their advisers.

Tom Bradley, then the mayor of Los Angeles, came to visit and responded enthusiastically to everything he saw. Soon after, during a visit to the West Coast, Philip Johnson stopped by our model shop. In his usual quick-witted manner, he asked questions, cracked jokes, and made sharp observations. One of his comments proved particularly insightful: "It seems to me there are too many trees," he said quite suddenly. "Trees are different from architecture. There aren't any trees at the Acropolis. How are you going to see your buildings?" As it happens, the Center now has far fewer trees at the top of the hill than were originally shown on the 1990 model.

By this stage, substantial decisions about landscaping could not be further postponed. Influenced, no doubt, by our earlier visits to Italy, I always imagined a fairly verdant setting for the Getty Center. We had all been extremely impressed by the gardens of the Villa Lante and the Villa d'Este and, while we were not going to replicate such works, we were more or less agreed on creating a kind of Italianate garden running down the central spine. But the amount of greenery on the site itself was a less urgent question than stabilizing the slopes in preparation for the onslaught of mechanical excavation and construction. The landscaping of the flanking slopes would also influence how the Getty Center would be perceived when viewed from afar, not least by Brentwood's vigilant homeowners.

The resolution of the landscape issue turned out to be far more complicated than I or anyone else had anticipated. Our initial landscape architect, Emmet Wemple, by then well into his seventies, seemed unable to devote his full energy to the task. And I had had my own ideas about the landscape, which were contradictory to those of Wemple. As a result, Steve Rountree and I recommended to Williams that we should employ another landscape architect. In 1990 we asked Dan Kiley, a doyen of American landscape design, to take over while keeping Wemple as a consultant.

Permanent concrete culverts were constructed at regular intervals to channel the rainwater along the contours of the eastern side of the site overlooking the San Diego Freeway.

In Kiley's view, Wemple's attempt to re-create a "natural environment" would undermine any sense of order on the slopes surrounding the site. I remember his asking me, "Don't you want something more structured?" This idea appealed to me because I appreciated the virtue of imposing an abstract order on such an undulating and unruly site. "Instead of just putting up trees as if you're turning your back and throwing pebbles over your shoulder," Kiley suggested, "let's create a certain order to the land." Together we developed the idea of planting the slopes with California live oaks in a regular pattern that related to the grid of the complex. Additional fire-retarding ground cover of poverty weed would then be added, consolidating the overall green image of the area and at the same time stabilizing the slopes.

The Getty building program committee accepted Dan Kiley's redesign as a brilliant breakthrough that represented a totally new approach, moving from the Romantic English to a much more classical and controlled French tradition. Soon after his plan had received approval, hundreds of saplings were planted on the eastern slope of the hill. But, unfortunately, Kiley was unable to win over the entire Getty team to the brilliance of his design. A septuagenarian, he had a quizzical, irreverent, and opinionated temperament, befitting an anarchic classicist from Vermont. I was delighted to be working with him, but this enthusiasm was not shared by the Getty. I argued that he was one of the best landscape architects in the world—a true master in his field—and that he had brought coherence to the landscape in a way that no other landscape architect could have done. But I failed to convince the building program committee and I was left with no choice but to begin the search all over again.

Our third landscape consultant was the Philadelphia-based Laurie Olin, who joined the team in 1993 and was to stay with us through the end of the project. It was not easy for him to pick up after so much had been put in place. But he responded in a sensitive way to the challenge. In most of the areas both outside and within the hilltop complex, he followed Kiley's ideas, but in a few areas he developed his own decidedly different approach, such as the randomly organized and varied cactus garden in the South Promontory. We worked well together, and, more important, he won and retained the confidence of Williams, Walsh, and Rountree.

Even more important than landscaping to the Center's eventual appearance was the selection of the external facing materials. In the 1987 agreement between the Getty and the Brentwood Homeowners' Association, we had already made a series of commitments about external finishes; these were confirmed when I met the board of trustees in September 1988. Notably, it was stipulated that the Center would be covered partly with stone and partly with another material, most probably metal panel. But the debate about the choice, texture, and cost of these materials would continue for years.

In February 1990, I informed the building program committee of my research into possible cladding solutions for the Center. I noted that all the buildings except the museum and the auditorium would require liberal amounts of glass, both to admit natural light and to provide views. I recommended that we use a metal panel with an enameled matte finish as a cladding for all the solid exterior walls that were not to be covered with stone. I had had extensive experience with different kinds of metal panel systems, including unfinished aluminum and porcelain-enameled steel, and by now I had confidence in their use. From the Bronx Developmental Center on, I always found such systems to be practical, reliable, attractive, and relatively inexpensive. Metal cladding seemed to be the right answer here as well. As I wrote in my report: "Like stone, this material is durable and permanent, and it will lend a uniform scale to the buildings it will cover. But the panels have a particular advantage in cladding these structures: they can easily be molded to fit the buildings' fluid sculptural forms."

I argued that the matte finish would emphasize the light, transparent qualities of the buildings, without being highly reflective or shiny. I felt the panels would not only complement the glass and stone employed elsewhere in the Center but also reflect the greens and blues of the surrounding landscape and the sky. It was, of course, understood that the metal panels would not be white, but I was equally determined that they should be of a light color. Michael Palladino prepared samples in fifteen different shades, which were then shown to the Brentwood Homeowners' Association. But it proved impossible to satisfy them. They would say the samples were too light, too dark, too green, too blue, too gray, and so on. The litany of their objections was endless. I realized that sooner

92

or later we would need to end this debate, yet the Getty was ever hopeful of winning them over through negotiation. Thus our consultations with the homeowners continued without any resolution throughout the spring of 1990.

On July 6 we had an early evening meeting with Bill Krisel and Bob Barnett, two architects who were representing the Brentwood residents, at the home of May Friedman, who was also a member of the Brentwood Homeowners' Association. Rountree and I showed two panels, one white and the other the warm gray that we had painstakingly selected. We soon began squabbling about what was and was not white. The meeting dragged on until two in the morning over many cups of coffee and an abundant selection of pastries. Despite the hospitality, it was an exercise in futility. Krisel and Barnett, it seemed to me, wanted to impose their own aesthetic criteria upon us in the name of "the people," meaning the residents of Brentwood.

After this marathon session I decided I had had enough, and I asked my associate Don Barker to take over. I knew that he could deal with Krisel and Barnett with more equanimity. And, to my delight and relief, I never had to meet with them again. Rountree and Barker finally negotiated an agreement in which they accepted a light beige panel that we had selected, which was very close to the color of the stone we ended up using.

Choosing the stone for the exterior was no less crucial, since it would ultimately be one of the most important factors in defining the Center's character. In my materials statement of February 14, 1990, I noted that a richly textured stone would suggest "permanence, solidity, simplicity, warmth and craftsmanship and would offer a connection to the land that no other material can provide." We began collecting stone samples from all over the world. And as the word spread of our likely needs, we were approached by a good number of stone merchants. At one point, I think we had assembled almost two thousand samples. From this huge number we selected some two hundred stones that were submitted to us in three-foot-square slabs. We lined them up in our model shop for inspection and began picking samples from which to make a final choice.

Some trustees favored a rough beige sandstone from Texas, but the stone was too soft and, in any case, I felt it was inappropriate for Los Angeles. Some attractive stones were either too expensive or not available in the quantity required. I remember flying over the Grand Canyon on my way to Los Angeles and thinking that the rock of the canyon had a particularly magical texture that responded to the warm tone of the light with heightened intensity. I also looked at Jerusalem stone because it had a color that reflected light in a unique way. But Jerusalem stone is available only in a fairly limited size, because of its geological formation and the method of quarrying, and also because of its softness and fragility. We looked at American granite and also at Indian sandstone, which had the great attraction of being the least expensive on the market. We even sent someone from our staff to accompany representatives of the Getty and the contractor on a week's visit to India to see if a sufficient amount could be delivered efficiently and on schedule. Their report was discouraging.

One day I was visited in my office in Los Angeles by Carlo Mariotti, an Italian who owns a large quarry in Bagni di Tivoli, just north of Rome. And, needless to say, he was keen to sell us his travertine. Up to this point, I confess, travertine had never interested me, perhaps because it is the stone most used in lobbies across America in the form of a thin veneer, as if it were wallpaper. But Carlo was insistent. "What if we could find a different way of using travertine?" he asked.

"The only way it would interest me," I told him, "is if we could use it in a very rough form, much as it was used in ancient times, in large pieces that would provide an aura of solidity."

Naturally we were not intending to deploy stone in the antique manner of solid coursed masonry; we merely wanted to clad a modern steel-and-concrete building with stone panels. However, we did want the Center, above all the retaining walls and the exterior of the museum, to have a certain sense of permanence. We were sent various samples of travertine with a rough, cleft finish and at last I felt we were moving in the right direction.

To my surprise, the Brentwood residents' group seemed quite happy with the choice of travertine, but Williams and Rountree needed more persuading. Worried about cost, they were still considering using stucco rather than stone, something I strongly opposed. "I am convinced that in the long run stone will be much less expensive than stucco," I told them at one meeting. They also worried about erosion and maintenance, not least because I wanted to use travertine for paving as well as cladding. "You spill a glass of wine and the whole thing is blotched," Rountree suggested. "But go to Rome," I pleaded. "Look at Rome. It is entirely built of travertine." Despite his reservations, Williams agreed to show the travertine sample as well as the beige metal panels to the board of trustees. But the debate was far from over. In September 1990, in the course of another cost-reduction panic, the draconian decision to eliminate all stone was almost taken without my full knowledge.

It soon became apparent that our plans to unveil our design to the press in October 1990 were far too optimistic. Aside from the unresolved question of the exterior finishes, I had to redesign the Research Institute for the History of Art and the Humanities as a result of a fundamental revision of the institute's program by Kurt Forster and his staff. Our first design reflected a more orthodox concept of a study center built around a central reading room, with separate offices for scholars. But Forster and his team decided to abandon the traditional library format in favor of an assembly of what they called resource spaces, in which each scholar would be literally surrounded by the material pertinent to a given project. As a result, the design became more open, with a cylindrical spatial organization arranged around a series of ramps descending from one level to the next.

In the end, the Research Institute may be the most innovative building of the entire complex, sort of a Guggenheim of books inspired by the spiraling gallery space of the Guggenheim Museum in New York. By virtue of its circular, ramped organization, this construction effectively invents a new building type inasmuch as the space of the lower two floors is broken up only by median-height, radial partitions stacked with books. This arrangement means that a single researcher or research team can, within limits, appropriate all the shelf space needed for a given project. And unlike a traditional library, the entire library here is treated virtually as a reading room.

While ramps lead into the two lower floors, visitors can also reach all five floors of the buildings by elevator and stairs. The upper floors, which open onto a central patio and the top-lit cylindrical space below it, contain private studies, meeting rooms, and offices, many of which have

A portion of the arroyo area after the
regrading and restabilization of the
soil had been completed prior to
the planting of the three thousand
California live oaks.
Opposite: The louvered construction
in the middle is the roof of the subterranean area containing the mechanical cooling towers for the complex;
Century City and downtown Los
Angeles are in the distance.

The vegetation on the site included chaparral shrubs and California live oaks. Only a few of the trees were large enough to be preserved; these were dug up, boxed, and held until their final position was determined.

their own terraces looking out over the site from different points. A wing of scholars' offices made up of four separate studies on two floors spreads out onto the ridge with a bridge linking it to the cylindrical "doughnut" of the library itself. A sunken courtyard is on the western side of this building, which also has a 120-seat lecture hall and a scholars' lounge.

Meanwhile, the myriad meetings I attended during my monthly visits to Los Angeles were consumed by discussions of everything from the color of the tram to the acoustics of the auditorium, from the integration of the antiseismic structure to the provision of adequate drainage throughout the site. In fact, the more we advanced from concept to reality, the more people appeared to offer advice. While certain outside views could be subtly assimilated into the design or even discreetly ignored, the rulings of the fire department were mandatory. The terms of the conditional use permit obliged the Getty to build a helipad close to the main buildings of the Center so that emergency firefighting helicopters could refuel and be recharged with water. At the insistence of the fire department, we even had to redesign the access ramp from the entry plaza to the museum to accommodate a fire truck.

Throughout 1990, the budget remained a sore point for all concerned. In May of that year Williams held a meeting in our conference room to discuss the problem. Looking back over the previous decade, he recalled that when the trustees took over after the death of J. Paul Getty, the museum was the Getty's only program. Since it was no longer possible to build a comprehensive collection of twentieth-century art, the trustees decided to create a new center devoted to the understanding of art in general. Williams reminded us that the Research Institute for the History of Art and the Humanities would have the finest art history resources in the world and went on to observe that the Conservation Institute already had the finest scientific staff anywhere. When the Getty decided to unite its programs in a comprehensive center, he added that he could not believe that a site like this could exist. After this diplomatic, morale-building résumé, he then addressed the question of money, noting that, while the Getty's endowment stood at around $3.3 billion, gross earnings of 9.25 percent to 10 percent annually were needed to earn the 5.3 percent in real interest necessary to finance the programs. After the October 1987 Wall Street crash, he said, sluggish markets made such a performance difficult to achieve. Finally, Williams got to his point and delivered his message that the endowment was for the programs and that the budget for the building program was final. There would be no more money.

The problem was that the cost estimates for the building kept on growing—from $600 million in September 1988 to $640 million, then $690 million, and now, according to the latest estimate by Dinwiddie, topping out at a grand total of $789.5 million. With each budget crisis, the possibility of having to redesign the entire Center returned. On September 6, 1990, I attended a construction budget meeting in which Rountree conveyed Williams's latest thoughts. He had offered four possible options: to do everything possible, short of a major redesign, to reduce the budget to $690 million; to do a large-scale redesign (I had already somewhat grudgingly accepted that the museum could be incorporated into a single building); to abort the project entirely; and finally, to keep the current design, put the current construction schedule on hold, complete all the working drawings and put them out to bid. This last, however, was an option that Williams did not really consider viable.

We sat around disconsolately discussing possible cost reductions, from eliminating the tram to relocating the food service facilities under the temporary exhibition building pavilion, to replacing 40 percent of the proposed stone revetment with a stucco finish. Dave Margolf, the construction cost consultant to the Getty, said he could reduce the budget to $735 million. Unbeknownst to me, Dinwiddie was already preparing a detailed alternative budget proposal, which I received in New York on September 11, 1990, along with the copy of a memorandum from Rountree echoing Williams's view that stone was altogether too expensive to face the museum's exterior. I was stunned. I picked up the telephone and called Williams to express my dismay at having been kept in the dark about these fundamental changes to the architecture, which were evidently being proposed by the cost consultants and the contractor without my knowledge.

In this adversarial atmosphere, a new and prolonged budget battle began. I asked all our technical consulting firms to propose additional

*The first California live oaks are
planted on the eastern slope according to the grid plan of landscape
architect Dan Kiley.*
Opposite: *A mound of excavated earth
was temporarily stacked where the
Research Institute would be built
above the fully planted arroyo; this
was the last part of the site to be built
upon so the earth was stored here.*

savings while I also continued to look for ways of cutting costs without affecting the quality of the work. Early in October, Williams received a revised estimate of $733 million, but this did little to abate the crisis. I was beginning to despair. In November 1990 I drafted a letter to the board of trustees in which I asked to attend their next meeting so I could present my case against the cost reductions now being proposed to the Getty by Karsten/Hutman Margolf in collaboration with Dinwiddie.

I never sent the letter, since I eventually was able to make Williams realize that to replace the stone and metal revetment with stucco would destroy the external appearance of the building. I conceded that some savings could be made by eliminating stone on some of the exterior retaining walls and by using Sheetrock with a skim-coat finish instead of plaster throughout the Center. However, I went on to stress that the proposed cladding of stone and metal paneling should be kept on the exterior of buildings, as well as on the interior finishes such as floors, portals, and stairs. I told him that "the exterior enclosure cannot be rebuilt at a later date when the substituted stucco exterior is inevitably cracked and crumbling. It is my fear that the institution that we think we are creating together would not be the one we will see six years from now."

In the months that followed, a new budget was established. In March 1991, the final design—a monumental package of design development documents and drawings—was approved by the Los Angeles Planning Commission. The following month, the same package was approved by the Getty's board of trustees. All the external finishes now had the board's approval and in effect we had the green light to start preparing the documents for construction.

We now had to face up to the tectonic and technical consequences of deciding to face large sections of the complex in cleft stone fastened to both a skeleton steel frame and in-situ concrete walls. I had substantial experience in cladding a steel frame with metal panels, but I had never used stone in this particular way before nor, as far as I could see, had anybody else. I wanted to use stone cladding sufficiently thick to convey the phenomenal weight and gravity of the material. I did not want to simulate the appearance of bonded masonry, which because of the ready availability of thin stone veneer had become so common in late modern

One of several sample cladding mock-ups from November 1991 that presented contrasting samples of metal panels and stone. The mockup above shows a beige metal panel and Indian sandstone that was being considered, and the bottom image is of the cleft-cut Roman travertine cladding that was selected after an exhaustive search.

A tent was erected on the site for the presentation of the design to the press in October 1991.

architectural practice. In short, I had set myself the contradictory task of using stone in such a way that one would be aware of both its weight and thickness *and* of its non-load-bearing status as a rain screen. We had to find a way of cutting the stone so it would match the thirty-inch-square metal panels used throughout the rest of the building. It proved difficult to find a stone-cutting machine capable of meeting this requirement, but we eventually succeeded. There was a good deal of discussion as to whether we could use open-jointed, stack-bonded stone in this way as a permeable rain screen, but eventually we succeeded in doing so, water-proofing the basic fabric on its outer surface with an air space separating it from the stone cladding. The rain would then pass through the stone and drain inside the cavity.

At last, on October 9, 1991, we gathered to unveil the final design to the press. It was a glorious morning and about two hundred people arrived at the hilltop site for the long-awaited occasion. Inside a giant white tent pitched on the very site where the museum would finally be built, we exhibited drawings and a wonderful twenty-eight-foot-long wooden model of the complex. This was the largest model we had built to date. Williams and Rountree spoke of a dream becoming reality, while I gave a talk explaining the principles governing the design. The model seemed to be a source of fascination, but suddenly we felt a kind of vulnerability. Up to now, the project had been exclusively ours; now the world could start giving opinions about what we had done or, perhaps, had failed to do.

There was a huge amount of press coverage, most of it simply descriptive of the project. I was more interested in the reactions of architecture critics and, of course, I was not always gratified by their opinions. "Can the Getty Buy Design Happiness?" was the headline of an article in *The New York Times* by Paul Goldberger. He wrote, "Mr. Meier's design, which calls for a campus-like arrangement of six similar but not identical structures, is serious and engaging, but without any single transcendent element, without any powerful, unifying architecture." Despite our long friendship, I felt that the scale and complexity of the project had possibly eluded Paul and that his perceptions seemed unclear at best.

On the other hand, Kurt Andersen of *Time* was one of the first to acknowledge that I had indeed broken away from the former, supposedly stereotypical limits of my "white" style. Thus, despite Andersen's misreading of the proposed finishes, I was more than a little pleased to read:

> Overall, the stucco and cleft-cut stone will give the Getty a nice grittiness lacking in Meier's previous work. Instead of the usual aloof Meieresque facades, the buildings are full of verve; they are even a bit manic. Instead of sleek uninterrupted planes of metal and glass, there are balconies, loggias and shady brise-soleils. If the new Getty becomes a lively, civilized place, it will be because, for all the white-on-white elegance, it is not pristine and hermetic, not another gorgeous monolith. The rugged terrain and Meier's good planning sense have dictated a dense urban messiness, with odd angles and almost ungainly juxtapositions, rather than some prissy classical grid over which buildings as jewels are dispersed just so.

For all of us involved in the project it was a moment of euphoria. The design had been thoroughly developed, the construction budget had been resolved, the Brentwood Homeowners' Association had been reassured, the fire and building departments had been satisfied, the grading and planting of the peripheral landscape was proceeding, and the city was on our side. It had been a bruising experience, but we had made it this far. Now all we had to do was build it. One month later, I wrote to Williams proposing an inauguration date for the Getty Center: October 12, 1996, which as it happened would have coincided with my sixty-second birthday.

Chapter 5

The Construction Emerges

It was now 1991, seven years since I had begun work on the project. The public unveiling of the design had brought us a brief respite, but now we had to take a deep breath and resume the marathon. Not everyone would stay the course. In spring 1990 Luis Monreal stepped down as head of the Conservation Institute to become the director of the cultural program of La Caixa Bank in Barcelona. He was replaced by Miguel Angel Corzo, a witty and dynamic art historian from Mexico. Sadly, two years later, Kurt Forster accepted a tenured professorship in the architectural history department of the Federal Institute of Technology in Zurich. His deputy, Thomas Reese, would serve as a very capable interim head of the Research Institute for the History of Art and the Humanities until January 1994, when Salvatore Settis took over as director. These changes meant establishing new relationships, but as far as the project was concerned power primarily remained concentrated in the hands of Harold Williams, Stephen Rountree, and John Walsh.

In my Los Angeles office, where there were now over seventy architects, parallel changes were occurring. A considerable turnover of staff pointed to a certain burnout and lowered morale. It was hardly surprising that young architects should grow bored with detailing endless fire stairs, doors, windows, and other seemingly mundane elements for months or even years on end. Throughout this period, Michael Palladino was a pillar of strength, not only commanding the office efficiently and attending countless meetings with the Getty staff while I was away, but also maintaining his habitual calm even when under intense pressure. In this regard, our temperaments complement each other perfectly: while I tend to react in a spontaneous and altogether rather unambiguous way, Michael maintains a more discreet and measured response to almost every situation.

It was an exceptionally busy time for me. While our Los Angeles office continued with the Getty commission, our New York office was engaged in designing the City Hall and Library for The Hague, the Canal+ television headquarters in Paris, and the Museum of Contemporary Art in Barcelona. This imposed a considerable strain on both me and the staff because, in addition to my monthly commute between New York and the West Coast, my European projects required regular trips to Europe. In Los Angeles, Palladino and I won an invited competition for the design of the new Museum of Television & Radio in Beverly Hills, a project that gave us great pleasure and only took two years to complete. Yet, whether I was in Los Angeles, New York, or Paris, it was the Getty Center that was always uppermost in my mind.

In Los Angeles I became reacquainted with former East Coast colleagues such as Frank Israel, Richard Weinstein, and Tim Vreeland, all of whom had moved out West long before my arrival. They introduced me to the leading architects of the Los Angeles scene and to other local luminaries. In fact, it was at a dinner party given by Tim and Nancy Vreeland that I met the designer Rose Tarlow, who was transforming the old Jack Warner estate for David Geffen. Rose became an important part of my life and she is one of the best things that came out of the experience of living and working in Los Angeles.

The constant travel between New York and Los Angeles and between New York and Europe led me back inadvertently to an earlier mode of artistic production. While I had indulged in making the odd collage ever since abandoning my larger and more naive ambition to become a painter-architect, I had never found time to produce a great deal of work. I framed the best of my collages, hanging them in my home or

Two views of the excavation, in September 1991, for the six-story underground parking structure located at the entry to the site
Overleaf: *View of the final model of the entire project done at quarter-inch scale between July 1991 and December 1993. This model consisted of seventeen models fastened together. When it is fully assembled, as shown here, it measures 17 × 37 × 5 feet. Because of its size, the only space big enough to photograph it properly was a soundstage at Paramount Studios.*

giving them to friends and on very rare occasions exhibiting them. Around 1980 all this changed as I began to fly regularly over continental distances. The inescapable boredom of air travel prompted me to devise a collage-making box carefully made to fit conveniently onto an aircraft flip-up table. Into the box went everything I needed for collage production, from glue and paint to scissors and cards, along with sundry typographic and photographic fragments that I had salvaged from everyday life. Along with colored paper, this was the basic raw material. I found I could produce five collages in a single flight from New York to Los Angeles and even more on trips to Europe and the Far East.

It soon became evident that I could not continue to frame all these collages, so the question arose of how to keep them. I hit upon the idea of making books of collage, in much the same way as Le Corbusier had taken sketchbooks with him whenever he traveled. I settled on a standard format of thirty-six pages measuring nine-and-a-half-by-twelve-inches and methodically started to work my way through one book after another, never getting on a plane without my collage box and the current book; to date I have made over a thousand collages and have filled up more than thirty books with thirty-six collages in each. Since the salvaged printed matter constantly changes its character, much of it coming into my hands through the process of travel itself—invoices, admission tickets, hotel stationery, wrappers, and endless typographic bits and pieces culled from magazines and exhibition catalogues—the numbered and dated books have also now come to serve as a kind of nonverbal journal that I have kept for nearly twenty years, a Proustian assemblage, which serves as a reminder of this or that unique occasion, the passing of time, and the movement of colleagues and friends.

Despite the endless discussions with the Getty over design and cost, I felt no loss of enthusiasm for the project. And even if I was constantly on the telephone with Los Angeles, I would return to the West Coast with renewed energy. On each visit, as work advanced, I saw something new. I began to notice relationships in the project that were a surprise even to me, since no completed building is ever quite as you had imagined it would be. Perhaps it also helped that I would work in Los Angeles for close to two weeks of each month and then go to New York or Europe to deal with my other commitments.

With the press unveiling, the design process was ostensibly at an end. Since the Getty had decided to adopt the so-called fast-track method of construction, we were constantly revising, designing, and drawing while the building was under way, our dedicated staff keeping just a few paces ahead of the numerous engineering consultants and the contractor. The alternative would have been the conventional approach of finalizing all construction documents before breaking ground, but this would have added at least two years to the estimated date of completion and occupancy. The fast-track approach nonetheless spawned a never-ending scramble, because constant cost-cutting measures and unforeseeable programmatic changes kept forcing us to redraw our original designs. One such change, for example, involved reworking the visitors' approach from the tram stop and entry plaza to the main entrance of the museum. All these changes added thousands of sheets to the drawings already under review and often entailed revision of the detailed construction documents required by different subcontractors involved and from the fabrication of the structural framework, the installation of heating and air conditioning, and the intricate detailing of the drainage and electrical infrastructure. In order to keep up with the extra work, I even added a second shift of about fifteen architects in my office, working exclusively on computer-generated drawings.

While architects are often thought of principally as designers, it was the act of building rather than just drawing that first drew me into the profession. For me, from the very beginning, this was what it was all about, and my feelings have not changed in thirty-five years. During the early months of construction at the Getty, I would climb to the highest point of the site just to watch the synchronized choreography of bull-dozers, earthmovers, and graders at work. I came to love the roar of their engines and eventually got to know most of the drivers of these monstrous vehicles. As they opened up the ground, I envisioned the Center's final form rising out of the void. In fact, because of the demands of the program and the height restrictions, three levels—nearly half the building—were entirely underground. The resulting excavation was immense, stretching some three hundred yards from the auditorium at

Lower parking garage excavation with my son, Joseph, attempting to give it a sense of scale

A view of the reinforced concrete lower level under construction in May 1994.
Opposite above: *By February 1995 more than half of the complex began to assume the outline of its final form in skeleton steel framework. The museum buildings are in the middle ground, the trust office and auditorium are in the distance.*

Opposite below: *The museum court-yard and the skeleton steel-frame enclosure of the temporary-exhibition gallery and entry rotunda are visible in April 1995.*

117

the northern end of the campus to the southernmost gallery of the museum.

As I repeatedly learned with this project, every advance seemed to be followed by a corresponding setback. Thus, my excitement over the start of construction was soon deflated by a resurgence of the budget crisis. While it was true that I was determined to maintain the quality of the building, I was not doing this out of vanity but out of a sense of commitment to the trustees' vision of the Center. At the same time, as early as 1985, the Getty had made clear to me that I had no say in decisions relating to the cost of construction. The Getty alone would determine its priorities as to what it wanted to spend and how it wanted to spend it.

At a meeting on February 10, 1992, Harold Williams said he was delighted with the design, but he then warned that we might be facing the worst depression since World War II, and this meant that his budget was now frozen. He also suggested that I appoint a new senior manager to keep down the cost of construction. Don Barker and Jim Crawford in my office would come to share this role. On March 6 Williams followed up his warning with a letter telling both Rountree and me that "we do not have a project unless we make substantial cost reductions." And he repeated his suggestion that we substitute stucco for the stone and the metal cladding. His letter ended rather pointedly: "We will get the best results from a collaborative effort. We do not need adversaries. We need partners."

A fresh memorandum from Williams just four days later was aimed even more directly at me. "It has been clear that you have not been willing to deal with cost issues constructively," he wrote. "While I can understand your desire to fight for design elements, this has led to an environment where we are adversaries rather than on the same team when it comes to cost. This has to change."

I was both surprised and affronted by this, for I felt I had always cooperated in the cost-cutting operation, even if I had not embraced it with the greatest enthusiasm. More to the point, the budget inflation was totally outside my control. In previous years, constant underestimation of costs by the Getty's own experts and the construction manager resulted in endless readjustments. Now, as the subcontracts were negotiated, the

Getty was forced once again to revise its cost estimates upward and, at the same time, to look for new savings. Worse would soon follow, as subcontractors who had committed themselves to a fixed price began returning to the Getty to claim they needed to charge more for their work. In the case of the tram, for instance, a contract price of $6 million inexplicably grew to $12 million. On the metal-panel exterior wall, the accepted bid price of $40 million increased to over $110 million. On-site security equipment, at one time estimated by Dinwiddie to cost $4 million, ended up costing ten times more. It was, at times, very frustrating and extremely difficult to get to the bottom of these increasing costs. I knew that the Getty was constantly setting ever higher standards for mechanical services and security systems, but one also had the feeling that the contractors' profit margins were equally susceptible to escalation.

In hindsight, it is clear that, having depended on me throughout the design process, the Getty management team now wanted to reduce my role. I had been involved in lengthy discussions with Walsh about the interior of the museum galleries; these talks had covered everything from theoretical and conceptual issues to questions about where specific paintings would eventually be hung. Then in 1992 Walsh decided, with Williams, Rountree, and the trustees immediately concurring, that the museum's decorative-arts collection should be displayed in rooms re-created in an eighteenth-century French style. And since this was evidently not something for me, Thierry Despont, the well-known New York–based French architect and interior designer, was hired to produce this effect.

Understandably, I was not enthusiastic. I did not believe decorative arts needed an Old World setting; they seemed perfectly at home without it in both my Frankfurt and Atlanta museums. But Walsh and his staff felt equally strongly about their view, and in the end I found that I was able to collaborate with Despont in a fairly amicable way. Along with Donald Kaufman and Taffy Dahl as color consultants, he proved extremely adept in dealing with the museum curatorial staff through the prolonged process of selecting the color and texture of the wall fabrics and other finishes to be applied to the galleries throughout. At the time of Despont's appointment, however, I saw this move as yet another sign of the Getty's shrinking faith in me.

The state of the construction during
1994. The reinforced concrete lower
levels were being built while the steel
reinforcement and formwork were in
preparation, and the skeleton steel
structure was being framed out.

Although the construction was proceeding at breakneck speed throughout 1994, due to the fast-track
method of construction, we were still
drawing the building details to stay
ahead of the contractor.

The imposition of another designer might not have been important, but Williams had just told me that he wanted Dan Kiley replaced as the landscape architect. The Getty had also named a local architect to design a maintenance and warehouse building at the foot of the hill on the eastern side of the site. On top of this, Williams was dissatisfied with our estimated fee for architectural work during the construction process. His complaint about our proposed interior design even led the Getty to consider involving another architect in choosing the furnishings of some of the office, laboratory, and library spaces. We were clearly losing the confidence of the client. In a letter dated May 19, 1992, Rountree said there was fear that "one program's offices would look pretty much the same as another's" if they all reflected my basic aesthetic. "Frankly, given the concerns, I am not sure it is possible for you to succeed in every space," he wrote. "It may be best for you to focus on the most public buildings."

There was evidently a communication problem, for which I had to share responsibility. However, while the Getty believed I was being stubborn and uncooperative, I felt that I had become the whipping boy for all the anxieties and frustrations resulting from the Getty's struggle to develop and refine its programs and, simultaneously, contain construction costs. In our own office, morale reached an all-time low. We were all groping, feeling our way forward in the dark, hoping that our version of the dream would materialize. But since every night brought a different dream, the expression of one dream would be criticized in the light of the next new aspiration. It was an immensely trying period for everyone. We had set off along the road toward the final goal but, although we were already in the construction phase, we still seemed uncertain about where we were going.

My response to the criticism was to sharpen the efficiency of our office and to attempt to be as accommodating as possible in my dealings with the Getty. The alternative was to walk away from the project, but I had already invested far too much time, energy, and passion to consider such a thing. Williams now engaged Joe Cutcliffe, an experienced work therapist who had already been consulting with the Getty staff and had been helpful in resolving some of their own internal difficulties. Cutcliffe's brief was to serve as a sort of marriage counselor to defuse tensions among my office, the Getty, and Dinwiddie. I was skeptical when I first talked to him over lunch, but in the long run he proved very helpful, suggesting a series of semi-autonomous teams to handle different problems and to try to accelerate decision making. Slowly, the crisis began to ease. And eventually, after prolonged discussions, my contract with the Getty was renegotiated and it was confirmed that no other architect would be appointed for the interior design.

But in one crucial area, I suffered a major setback. As early as March 1992, John Walsh had questioned the landscape design for the area we had created known as the central garden. This was the major outdoor public space in the complex located between the museum and the Research Institute. In a memorandum to Williams. Walsh suggested that the Getty should start from scratch in this part of the site. Arguing that he had seen no horticultural poetry to date, he mentioned two possible approaches that would serve as metaphors for the overall philosophy of the institution. With one option, native California vegetation would be combined with species brought from around the world to create a mini–botanical garden; with the other, inspired by Granada's Alhambra Palace, he proposed irrigating the site with small watercourses that, originating in different parts of the site, would come together to symbolize the fusing of the Center's creative forces. Most alarming, though, he argued that the lowest level overlooking the orange grove should be developed by an artist.

It seemed to me that the Getty team was disturbed by the fact that, unlike the other parts of the institution, the form of the garden would not be defined by the Center's program and that this part of the complex was not under the jurisdiction of any particular department. This left the Getty team struggling to give meaning to the garden. It seemed to make them search for ways to bring control over this part of the project.

The main axis of the central garden was intended to serve as a spine binding together the three circular forms employed in the Center: the drum of the museum entry; the circular court of the Research Institute; and the circular reflecting pool that was to have been situated in the orange grove below the belvedere.

In effect we envisioned the central garden as major outdoor public space composed of a sequence of small-scaled areas, part planted, part paved, through which visitors would be able to promenade freely,

Top to bottom: *The work in progress from December 1994 to March 1995, and a view from the southern terrace of the museum*

In the spring of 1994 the auditorium took shape in a skeleton steel network framing dramatic views of the site and its surroundings.

descending past a series of pools and courts until they reached the loggia wall that connected the museum to the Research Institute; from this point they would have been able to overlook the entire city. We designed this landscape to provide a variety of situations suitable for discussion, contemplation, and relaxation, to be equally appropriate for individuals or large groups. We imagined the garden space as a foil to the internal complexity of the institutional structure: a space where tour groups could assemble, where small seminars and concerts could be held, where people could congregate or be alone enjoying the natural beauty of the site. It seemed to me to present a wonderful opportunity for realizing an Italianate garden in the benevolent California climate.

But it was not to be. Within a few months, the California artist Robert Irwin was appointed the designer of the central garden. I was duly invited to attend a meeting between Williams and Irwin on August 3, 1991, at which point Irwin wanted to know what was expected of him. The area where he was asked to create a landscape sculpture was pointed out to him, and he promised to spend some months thinking about the topography as well as getting a general feel for the site. He would then present his first idea to Williams, Walsh, and Rountree and, on the basis of their reaction, he would decide whether to accept the invitation to participate in the project or not.

I confess I was disturbed that an artist—any artist—had been brought in, because as far as I was concerned the central garden was an essential part of the architectural concept. In theory, Irwin was instructed to work with me, but in practice this proved impossible. Later, when Irwin was officially appointed, I was told that he would design "an original and unique site-specific work of art." Rountree informed me somewhat cautiously that "Bob understands that he has to have your enthusiasm and support."

I had no choice but to accept the Getty's decision, but I had difficulty in adjusting to Irwin's involvement, and also to the final character of his design. It soon became obvious to me that I was alone in my reservations: after the formal presentation of Irwin's design in May, Williams wrote to me expressing his enthusiasm for Irwin's piece. I tried to work with Irwin, not least because I wanted to retain control over the design of the rest of the central garden, where Williams

*The framing for the museum and the
museum entry rotunda, during the
spring of 1995*

agreed that we would provide trees, water, shade, and seating as well as open space.

The issue dragged on through the summer into the fall and beyond. In September, the Getty made clear that Irwin's responsibility was limited to the so-called ravine and the bowl area—that is, the lower part of the garden. While Rountree also confirmed my authority as the architect responsible for coordinating all aspects of the project, this proved impossible to reinforce. For a meeting on October 6, 1992, I prepared a drawing for Steve Rountree showing Irwin's latest design in the context of the Center's overall site plan. I expressed my concern that Irwin's design displayed little or no relationship to the basic concept. His scheme covered the area between the museum and the Research Institute, with a zigzag ramp contained by Cor-Ten steel plates. Irwin's ramp continued down the southern slope to terminate in a circular, mazelike pool, which was the core of the piece. I found the use of Cor-Ten equally distressing since I knew that this rust-colored, oxidizing steel often produces rather disfiguring effects on its surroundings.

By this time, Laurie Olin had replaced Dan Kiley as the landscape architect, and the Getty was happy with his general handling of the plant material. Understandably, Olin was not eager to be drawn into the debate. He knew that I was dissatisfied with Irwin's scheme, but he also knew that Irwin would accept no changes. Indeed, he was aware of the fact that his opinion on this issue probably carried little weight.

Finally, in April 1994, the dispute was settled. On April 6 I sent one last appeal to Williams, suggesting that the now disbanded design advisory committee be invited to review the alternative designs for the central garden. The committee could provide a forum, I wrote, "in which we may clear away the smoke, have a reasonable examination of the situation and put this issue to rest once and for all." Williams responded immediately, declaring that he had made an irrevocable decision to implement the Irwin scheme. He went on to express how much he respected my passionate concern about the matter, but nonetheless concluded by letting me know that the trust's objectives would be best achieved by proceeding with Irwin's design.

What was most difficult for me in this whole affair was that Irwin was being treated as an artist while I was being relegated to the secondary

In the summer of 1995, the framework of the museum galleries was in the process of being enclosed; this is the view of the museum entry rotunda from the courtyard.

status of architect. His creative work was regarded as sacrosanct and subject to only token cost control, while my contribution was fair game for everyone.

Only in retrospect have I come to understand why the Getty turned to an artist to design the lower part of the central garden—and it was not the only time. In May 1993, for instance, the artist James Turrell was asked to develop three site-specific pieces for the upper section of the central garden: a thirty-six-foot-square "skyspace," which was a columned room with an open roof; a so-called grotto piece, which was a blackened room with very little natural light; and finally, a glazed slot that illuminated a subterranean space beneath the garden. In the end, none of these proposals was realized, ostensibly on the grounds of their cost.

On March 7, 1992, long before Irwin's official appointment, Kurt Forster circulated a memorandum that amply reflected his own concerns about the landscape. He seemed particularly eager to give a strong identity to the Getty garden, even imagining a landscape that he called "a hidden center." He argued that the terracing and contouring of the garden should heighten the visitors' awareness of the movement and texture of the earth's surface, thereby evoking a sensibility that has been largely lost in our post-industrial age. He felt that the designer's task was to reveal the inner substance of the site, its elemental composition in terms of earth, water, and stone. He went on to say how he could well imagine an artist like James Turrell being called upon to create an observatory embedded within the garden to become a vantage point from which to view the constantly changing spectrum of the sky. While Kurt thought that the greatest weakness of the garden was its uniformity, and he even went on to introduce the name of Robert Irwin, he nonetheless felt that it was important not to allow the central garden simply to "peter out" into the ravine below as a consequence of eliminating the original loggia wall.

While this critique went some way toward articulating many of the Getty's reservations about my orthogonal approach to the garden, it also echoed an anxiety that I happened to share—namely, that the removal of the loggia wall would cause the garden to lose its topographic shape as it descended into the ravine. Thus, while I was willing to integrate a

132

site-specific work of art into the design of the garden. I did not want it to undermine the unifying character of the landscape design.

One problem with my early plan to make extensive use of water in the Getty gardens was that despite the Mediterranean character of the site, with its distant views over the Pacific, the Getty became fearful that excessive use of water might be seen as wasteful and ostentatious in the arid environment of southern California. Apparently, a modest amount of irrigation of lawns was one thing, the constant recycling of fountain systems quite another. The rather lavish fountains and water basin that had been initially projected for the site were therefore cut back to five discrete pieces of water. The first is the stepped cascade of water that runs beside the broad flight of steps connecting the entry plaza to the museum entrance. This cascade feeds directly into a long orthogonal pool, with fountain jets flanking the entry plaza, the noise of which welcomes the visitors on arrival. This acoustical effect helps create the sense that one has indeed arrived in a refreshing place. A similar Islamic feature appears in the upper central garden running along the western side of the museum compound and ending in a cone-shaped basin that empties into the lower central garden. Within the museum courtyard proper we devised a magnificent arcade of seventy jets vaulting to a height of seven and a half feet, inspired by fountains in the Alhambra Palace.

The fifth water piece is a large circular fountain and pool let into the southern end of the museum courtyard. This pool was strategically positioned so that it was not only on axis with the center of the entry rotunda to the north but was also on axis with the courtyard of the Research Institute to the west. In the tradition of Japanese and Chinese gardens the pool became an occasion for some free play with rock forms. But first we had to find the right kinds of rocks, and for that I turned to Laurie Olin, who knew of a rock nursery in Valley Springs, California. Laddie Flock, the proprietor of the rock nursery, seemed to understand what we were looking for. With Dennis Hickok of our staff and Laurie Olin outlining the design intent, he set up a sample cluster of mono-chromatic rocks in a specially prepared pool in the midst of a forest and, on behalf of the Getty, it was agreed to buy them on the spot. The rocks we selected were an off-white stone with subtle blue veins. We were told

The museum (opposite) *and the* Research Institute (above) *begin to emerge as solid structures; the cleft-cut travertine walls of the museum and the concrete undercroft of the Research Institute already indicate something of the buildings' final form.* Opposite below: *Two views of an anti-seismic reinforced concrete basement of the North Quad under construction, and* (left) *the museum rotunda skylight*

their soft curves had been formed by a weathering process that had taken thousands of years.

Soon almost thirty tons of the river rocks arrived on site and we began the intriguing and, at times, difficult process of trying to arrange the rocks the same way we had in the forest pool. It was a trying and time-consuming exercise, since this trial-and-error approach to composing with boulders required the constant presence of a crane and its operator. Finally positioned, the rocks were bedded in concrete within a shallow basin, some rocks being almost submerged and others being brought to life by the play of the water. The effect was not only visual but also aural and tactile, with the sound of fountains bringing a sense of coolness in the intense heat of summer.

Fortunately, despite all the conflict surrounding the central garden, the rest of the project was moving ahead quite smoothly. We had agreed that the North Quad buildings around the entrance plaza— that is, the auditorium, the trust offices, the Conservation Institute, the grant program, the Center for Education in the Arts, and the restaurant-cafeteria—would be finished and occupied while further construction work continued on the museum and the Research Institute. Nonetheless excavation work began throughout the site simultaneously since it was apparent that the museum would take the longest time to build, not least because its undercroft housed the mechanical services for the entire complex. The size of this excavation of course created enormous additional difficulties because of our commitment to the Brentwood Homeowners' Association not to remove any earth from the site.

Dinwiddie decided to build in a clockwise manner, starting with the North Quad, going on to the museum, and ending with the Research Institute. Soon there was a flurry of activity, building up over the next three years until nine hundred hard-hatted construction workers were on the site at any one time, handling earthmoving equipment, cement mixers, and huge cranes that carried steel columns, beams, and girders to and fro. Thousands of tons of concrete were used to build the foundations and underground areas. But until the steel framework began to enclose the spaces aboveground, it was difficult for anyone to perceive with any certainty the ultimate relationships among the buildings. Then, almost from one day to the next, the skeletal form of the entire complex began to appear, as if sketched out by an invisible hand against the sky. While I was staying on the site, I recall looking at the structure incredulously each day, on waking each morning, noticing how it was gradually being transformed. Moreover, from the freeway drivers could at last begin to believe that the Getty Center was indeed being built.

As the project advanced, a host of new, unexpected problems arose. In normal high-rise office buildings, four feet is usually allowed for the void between the suspended ceiling of a space and the floor above. This is the space reserved for electrical and mechanical equipment, along with structure, fireproofing, plumbing, and necessary sprinkler piping. Under our conditional use permit, we were restricted to a fifteen-foot floor-to-floor height in order to adhere to the overall forty-five-foot height limit, but even so we could still afford a ten-foot floor-to-ceiling height, with a so-called sandwich palette of five feet, one foot higher than the norm allowed in standard high-rise office construction. But the five feet proved tight because of special seismic requirements and the addition of the elaborate humidity and air temperature control systems specified by the Getty. Suddenly, our technical consultants had to rethink how everything would fit, including all the piped services required by the Conservation Institute's laboratories. And it did not help that antiseismic standards and other servicing requirements were being constantly upgraded as the job proceeded. Eventually, everything was squeezed in, but this was typical of the problems that kept surprising us throughout the process.

The fast-track construction approach also demanded exceptional coordination among the Getty, the architectural and engineering teams, and the construction manager, not least because of the cost-cutting struggle, which continued unabated. Every time an item was eliminated from the design, drawings had to be changed or modified. Many of the proposed savings related to future—as yet unbuilt—details and, where necessary and still possible, these revisions were integrated into the first construction documents.

One of the savings we considered was the reduction of the seismic criteria for the steel structure of the administration building and the special-exhibitions gallery. As fate would have it, barely six weeks later, on January 17, 1994, the Northridge earthquake struck Los Angeles, causing widespread damage. I was in New York at the time and was

Looking from the museum toward the
North Quad and Conservation Institute
beyond. The latter was already enclosed
with insulation prior to the application
of the metal paneling.
Opposite above: *View from the terrace of
the Conservation Institute to the museum.*
Opposite below: *Looking from the foundation of the Research Institute across to
the frame of the restaurant/café*

immediately called. The word was "There's no problem. Nothing happened here." Upon closer inspection, however, disturbing hairline cracks were discovered in the welds and plated joints of the steel framework. Fortunately, no cost-cutting measures had been implemented in this area, so they could hardly be seen as being responsible for the damage.

Until now our experience had been of horizontal seismic movement, and building codes had always been devised to resist this kind of stress. However, this particularly strong tremor was vertical. It damaged the off-site temporary library of the Research Institute, located in Santa Monica. The quake tipped all the books onto the floor and simultaneously set off sprinkler heads in the ceiling of the library space. Water rained down on the books, and the doors were difficult to open because volumes that had piled up helter-skelter on the floor blocked their operation. The doors had to be taken off their hinges, trailers immediately hired, and the books shipped in all directions to be freeze-dried in refrigeration plants as the first step in an emergency restoration procedure. Needless to say, this meant we had to reconsider the design of the bookshelves in the new premises for the Research Institute.

Fortunately, the fireproofing had yet to be applied to the steelwork of the Getty Center, so the fine fissures at the joints were readily perceived. But it was not immediately evident what should be done about these micro-failures. In the first place, all the joints had to be ultrasonically examined to determine the full extent of damage. The failure was particularly disconcerting since skeleton steel frames had long been considered one of the most reliably earthquake-resistant structures. Further, there was no consensus as to the best methods of repairing the damage and restoring the strength and durability of the connections. Never inclined to do things by halves—and certainly not now—the Getty Trust sponsored a crash research program, with the collaboration of the University of Texas, that simulated the effects of vertical earthquake movement on a great number of typical steel connections.

The test results put the blame on brittle weld metal and inadequate welding. A modified beam-to-column connection was therefore devised, wherein welded cover plates were added to the top and bottom beam flanges. This retrofitting procedure was adopted for the existing steelwork throughout the Getty site, while the connections in the framing of the two buildings still to be erected were redesigned to meet the new standards. The structural engineer, Robert Englekirk, recommended that a welding specialist be hired to completely review the welding specifications and quality control program. While a similar review had previously been done quite well at the Getty, he still felt that an independent review might lead to possible improvements.

By early 1994, the directors of the various programs were beginning to refine their interior furnishing requirements. So, with two talented and experienced interior designers, Christine Kilian and Rick Irving, who for some time had been an integral part of our staff, we were now able to differentiate and translate these specific requirements into precise and articulate designs. As far as the office spaces were concerned, the main issues were organization and the establishment of relationships among various departments and staff members. This affected the balance between individual and collective work spaces, as well as the provision of sufficient room for storage and ancillary equipment. Careful consideration had also to be given to the quality of both artificial and natural light, individual furnishings for specific work areas, and adequate storage for books and art. Since each area was designed for particular individual and group needs, there was no prototype that could satisfy everyone. Further, the glaring California light was a constant preoccupation, especially since so many people were now working with computers. As a result, some of the office spaces were equipped with venetian blinds in addition to the sunscreens that were already part of the exterior building fabric.

During this process, we developed a range of maple cabinetwork and furniture that, in my view, was as practical as it was attractive. However, on May 6, 1994, Rountree informed me that, while the architect could select furnishings for the public areas, including the auditorium, the lobby spaces, and the museum, the Getty would look after its own needs in offices, laboratories, shops, and library spaces. Once again, the reason given was budget, with Rountree saying he expected a good deal of the office furniture to come from existing stocks. Fortunately, things turned out differently. I told Rountree that we would still attempt to devise a range of furniture that covered the full gamut of

During construction, the arrival plaza was transformed by temporary reflecting pools when it was flooded to test the impermeability of its cover over the parking garage beneath.

the Getty's needs. As a result, Kilian and Irving set about interviewing nearly every Getty staff member about personal requirements. In the end, we designed or selected nearly all the furniture, carpets, blinds, and lights for the entire complex, including all of the museum and auditorium seating. Each desk and cabinet was designed for a specific space. It was an exercise in participatory democracy: every individual was consulted and, after lengthy deliberation, each micro-situation was finally resolved to everyone's satisfaction and pleasure. As a result, every office floor and department now has its own character and identity, recognizable at a glance.

With the museum, a whole proliferation of details had to be settled, and, in each case, there were always several points of view (although Walsh, as the museum's director, naturally had the last word). The height of the picture rail, for instance, took many months to define. We had many meetings about the natural light emanating from the painting gallery skylights—how this would change over a day, how artificial lighting could be made to approximate natural light, and how the color of the walls and wall fabrics would affect the overall perception of the ambient light. The floors of the painting galleries were always intended to be made of wood, but we still had to decide the color, size, grain, pattern, and finish of the flooring to be adopted. The display cases that would contain either delicate works on paper or small objects were also the subject of lengthy discussion, with the Getty eventually commissioning Thierry Despont to design them.

The year 1994 was not without its pleasures in other areas. With Frank Stella's encouragement, I had for the past two years been trying my hand in the field of welded sculpture, and these efforts attained some public recognition when I exhibited nearly fifty pieces at a one-man show that opened at the Leo Castelli Gallery in SoHo on September 17. The way in which these pieces had come into being was also very personal, inasmuch as Frank let me use some of his space at the Tallix Foundry in Beacon, New York. There I was also given an instant education in welding stainless steel by Dick Polich, the foundry director, and his technician, Michael Pilon. The raw material for these pieces were discarded wood fragments from our model shop in Los Angeles, which I later had cast into metal at the foundry. It was quite a business shipping all this junk back to New

144

York, but we managed one way or another. I was in the collage business again, only this time in a more substantial three-dimensional medium. As the scheduled date for the exhibition approached, I felt increasingly nervous, and I could not have pulled it off without my friend Earl Childress's criticism and assistance, and the advice I received from Leo Castelli about the format of the exhibition itself. The finishing touch was a beautiful catalogue designed by Massimo Vignelli.

By early 1995, while much work had still to be done on the museum and the Research Institute for the History of Art and the Humanities, the North Quad buildings were beginning to assume their final form. It was encouraging to be focusing at last on interior design, because it meant the end of the road was in sight. What was even more reassuring, in our monthly meetings with the Getty project management team, concern about delays in completing construction (Dinwiddie was by then several months behind schedule) had assumed greater importance than the perennial budget debate. At a meeting held on January 9, 1995, Harold Williams announced that the North Quad should be finished by March 15, 1996, that the museum would be completed no later than January 15, 1997, and that the Research Institute was to be completed two months later. Earlier, it had been estimated by the museum staff that ten months' installation time was needed between completion of construction and its formal inauguration, but nonetheless Williams maintained that the entire Center should be ready to open to the public by September 1997.

Subsequently, on February 24, 1995, we received a report from the Getty's scheduling adviser, Poulsen Construction Management, which made disconcerting reading since it revealed that almost every aspect of construction was behind schedule. Poulsen estimated that the North Quad would be completed only in May or June 1996. Consequently, Williams's target date for the completion of the museum had to be revised. The pace of construction work was stepped up and overtime was authorized; with this, the cost of the project began to escalate once more. But by now the Getty was thinking only of completing and occupying the entire facility.

At least once a month, in the early morning, I would walk over the

The helicopter pad is visible on the promontory to the left as one looks north from a window in the trust building.
Opposite: *The cafeteria opens onto the terrace and above it is the double-height restaurant space.*
Overleaf: *View from the terrace of the Getty Trust president's office looking toward the metal-clad Conservation Institute and the cleft-cut stone walls* of the eastern side of the museum galleries

entire site with the chief construction manager, Ron Bayek. Dedicated, enthusiastic, and deeply respected by the construction workers, he was one of the few senior members of the Dinwiddie staff who were engaged on the Getty Center for the full span of its realization. During our monthly tours, we touched on almost every aspect of the unforeseen minutiae that comes up on all construction jobs. We formed a good partnership: he often alerted me to critical situations of which I was unaware; in return, I was able to take action to ease some of his problems.

While the exterior of the North Quad buildings and the entry plaza were being completed, interior construction work was proceeding apace, including millwork, painting, carpeting, and the installation of equipment. Finally, in late spring 1996, the North Quad complex was ready for occupation. Now it was as if we had two Getty Centers, one with dazzling new buildings calmly grouped about a stunning plaza covered with travertine, the other still immersed in dust and noise and overrun by machines and workers. In the summer of that year, the Getty staff began to move into the North Quad, starting with the Conservation Institute in July. Many people were surprised. All the trials and tribulations, delays and difficulties, began to fade into the background. It was quite strange. People so used to complaining had no complaints; quite suddenly they were all genuinely happy.

On August 14, 1996, the day after the Getty Trust moved into the administration building, I received a most welcome letter from Steve Rountree in which he said he wanted to share with me the spontaneous positive reception given to the buildings. He described the genial, almost festive atmosphere of the buildings flooded with sunlight, and the staff strolling across the plaza from their respective offices. He reflected on the fact that we had been jointly engaged in this effort for twelve years and that it had proved more difficult than either of us had imagined. He concluded by saying that the positive reaction to the East and North buildings made it all worth it and that he and the Getty team were now looking forward to the completion of the museum and Research Institute with anticipation and confidence.

On the day Harold Williams moved into his new office overlooking the freeway, with its equally spectacular views of both the distant mountains and downtown Los Angeles, he, too, was overjoyed, brimming with pleasure not only for himself, but also for all the people who were there. I think it was an experience that he was unprepared for. There were parties, lunch get-togethers, staff gatherings. It was a moment of celebration—and this, needless to say, touched me profoundly. Now that the Getty personnel were moving in, I could at last begin thinking about the day when all the work would be completed—and my responsibilities would be fulfilled.

Chapter 6

The Grand Finale

As 1996 drew to a close, with the noise of Christmas parties in the North Quad competing with the roar of cranes echoing around the museum courtyard, the bulk of my work on the Getty Center was nearly complete. In fact, almost as if some secret destiny were confirming that this was indeed the last phase of the operation, I learned, early in December, that I was to be the 1997 recipient of the Gold Medal of the American Institute of Architects. I was deeply moved by this honor, which is bestowed by the profession annually on one of its members. It is normally reserved for architects at the end of their careers, even occasionally awarded posthumously. I felt enormously encouraged; while the Gold Medal is always awarded for a total body of work, it seemed plausible to assume that in this instance it was a form of recognition by my peers for the achievement of the Getty Center.

No less important to me was a very warm letter of recommendation that Harold Williams had written, on my behalf, to the AIA board of directors. The letter helped put the frustrations and difficulties I experienced in designing and realizing the Getty into some kind of perspective.

Throughout the job, innumerable incidents had generated tensions on both sides. Certainly I was not always the easiest architect to deal with. I tended to be obsessive about details, and I was often stubbornly convinced that my professional opinion was the only valid one in any given situation. More than once, Harold Williams must have despaired over my obstinacy. Yet, despite all our mutual difficulties, he was evidently proud of what we had achieved together. And in all probability, he, too, was pleased that the Getty Center should somehow be associated with the AIA Gold Medal.

All in all this was a wonderful note on which to enter into my final year at the Getty, yet as the opening approached I was still not ready to look back. In the early months of 1997, as I walked onto the site from the modest but rambling house that had long been my California home, I found myself observing a work very much in progress. The heavily textured stone façades of the museum were now well in place, but the temporary exhibition building and the Research Institute still looked like strange, steel-framed skeletons looming out of the ground, their final configuration awaiting the metal cladding in which they would be enclosed. Irwin's site-specific artwork, with its abundant rings of Cor-Ten steel, had been installed in its final position on the southern slope of the lower central garden, but the landscaping around it and in the area between the Research Institute and the museum was largely incomplete. With Dinwiddie's crews working overtime to meet the opening deadline, our old budget battles were totally forgotten. It was now officially acknowledged that the final cost of the Getty Center would be around $1 billion, but all that now seemed to matter was to complete the work in time for official inauguration on December 13, 1997.

In these last months, I was involved in adding final touches to what appeared to be an endless series of small details, such as the exact location of trees in the landscape, the design and location of exterior and interior furniture, and the addition of accents of color to certain interior spaces. Last but not least, I had to urge Dinwiddie to get all the fountains to function as they had been designed. The enormous corrective punch lists of work to be either completed or corrected by the contractor seemed never ending. These concluding rituals did not mean that I fretted less, for I was determined to maintain the quality of the construction

The tram station with its garden court and landscaping is the entry to the Getty Center at the lower level. Here, after leaving the subterranean garage, one gets a first glimpse of the campus on the crest of the hill.

*Two approaching views to the
campus from the northwest and
the north, showing the way in which
the serpentine tramway provides
constantly changing perspectives of
the site with the city lying beyond.*

and the level of the finish to the placement of the very last stone. Even now, at the eleventh hour, the job was still full of nerve-racking surprises. Typical of this was the shock we received when the contractor removed the scaffolding from the façade above the museum entrance. We were alarmed to discover a slight variation in the color of the metal panels that had been installed, and we had no choice but to re-erect part of the scaffolding and rectify the problem by replacing the faulty panels. Another small crisis occurred when the experts responsible for securing safe access for the disabled throughout the site concluded that the decomposed-granite walkways would be too soft for wheelchairs when the ground became wet. Once again, a substitution was necessary. I even flew to Rome to inspect a particular sample of travertine that we thought could replace the soft paving material. There was also the problem in some offices where members of the administrative staff complained of excessive sunlight falling onto their computer screens; in some places we had to install perforated blinds.

One of the most unusual situations arose with the finishing of the two small, high-ceiling "canon" galleries on the second floor. Here the sub-contractor had mistakenly painted the walls a single color instead of leaving the upper half white. I was delighted by this error, because the net effect was to unify the space. Ironically, John Walsh, who had so often resisted my notorious predilection for white surfaces, now objected to an entire wall of dark cerulean blue, arguing that a break between the upper and lower halves of the wall would give more intimacy to the lower hanging space. Once again we were at loggerheads, only this time he was arguing for white and I was advocating a solid color throughout. I once again lost the argument—for this, as I still had to learn, was a province where the curator's voice would always prevail.

This does not necessarily mean that curatorial taste is unimpeachable, as Italian architectural critic Francesco Dal Co reminded us in his sharp editorial commentary that appeared in the February 1997 issue of *Casabella,* when he wrote:

> Unfortunately someone at the Getty, struck by a dadaist whim, or simply an excess of bad taste, decided to assign the Franco-American interior designer Thierry Despont the task of decorating

the exhibition spaces designed by Meier—spaces that Meier conceived in keeping with the overall style of the entire "Getty-Acropolis." Fireplaces of undefinable origin, retro tapestries, plastic moldings, dentilated cornices, materials of questionable nobility, coquettish and brutal, and much more are generously employed by Despont to bring to life an astonishing scene of the dreams—or nightmares?—of a parvenu. The *Los Angeles Times* (July 25, 1996) declares that the décor is a purposeful confrontation between opposites. This is not so; if a word is needed to describe the situation, then, instead of "confrontation," "betrayal" or "infringement" would be more appropriate. If there is anything more remote (and opposite) from Meier's style, it is this explosion of vulgarity.

The furnishings of the museum's galleries would remain an ongoing controversy. We had ostensibly been hired as the architects for both exteriors and interiors, but a great deal of ambiguity arose once Thierry Despont was charged with the design of the period rooms for the decorative-arts collection. At this point, to head off further argument, Steve Rountree informed me that our jurisdiction extended to the internal public space of the museum, but for some inexplicable reason the galleries did not fall under this heading. My reluctance to accept this division of labor deepened after we were informed that the museum would be equipped with incidental furniture pieces designed by local artists and craftsmen. All at once a kind of spontaneous competition began between the contending parties—that is, between our designs for all the occasional benches, couches, tables, and chairs of the museum and the designs of various California cabinetmakers for similar items. The Getty eventually agreed to look at all the prototypical alternatives, and to my unanticipated gratification our version of the gallery furniture was finally chosen. Delighted, I telephoned John Walsh to tell him how much this meant to me and to Michael Palladino, Christine Kilian, Rick Irving, and all the other architects in my office who had worked so hard to perfect the pieces in question. We had gone out of our way to design furniture pieces that would suit the building and blend in with the rather traditional curatorial line being maintained in the museum as a whole. By using high-quality wood and leather upholstery we managed to pitch

The stone-clad ramp between the arrival plaza and the restaurant/café gives visitors an alternative route as well as providing fire-truck access to the museum.

*The tram station on the upper level
opens directly onto the arrival plaza.
Opposite above: Most visitors will
proceed up the grand stairway to the
museum.
Opposite below: A close-up view of
the museum*

163

the tone of our interior work somewhere between the modern American craft tradition, as exemplified, in part, by the furniture of Frank Lloyd Wright, and the more abstract modern tectonic tradition to which my architecture belongs. Despite this decision, however, the museum staff were still adding in their office spaces pseudo-Stickley tables and chairs that they had commissioned from a California craftsman.

By the summer of 1997, with the museum and a large portion of the Research Institute completed, the whole of the Getty Center began to be perceived as a finished work. Despite the fact that architects are practiced at visualizing their designs in advance, nothing compares to the satisfaction of seeing the conception become a reality. The interplay of spatial relationships is always something of a surprise, no matter how long or how intimately one has worked on a job. In this case, despite the myriad details that changed along the way, the complex's basic form and idea had been sustained. And as I watched it nearing completion, I felt confident that the form was appropriate, not only to the site but also to the mandate of the Getty.

For many, the high stone walls flanking the Center give it the air of a citadel, a monastery, or even an Italian hill town, but I know that it was never designed with such direct images and associations in mind. Admittedly, when viewed from below, along the San Diego Freeway, the stone facing does give the building a monumental presence, but this was not the original intention. On the western side, when viewed from Brentwood, the complex is more self-effacing and closely integrated into the landscape. I wanted to evoke the feeling of a campus, to give the arriving visitors a sense of intimacy and ready accessibility as they reach the entry plaza, as well as the sense that, with but a few steps, they could reach any part of the complex. Thus, from the very outset, the serpentine tram ride with its attendant landscape was meant to induce a sense of expectancy as the crest of the hill is approached. Visitors arriving by tram first glimpse the curved roof of the auditorium; then an instant later, they are swept past its undulating façade. Stepping out of the tram, they confront the curved form of the museum, with its cylindrical entry rotunda lying immediately behind it. Only after ascending the broad flight of steps leading up to the museum do they see the Research Institute lying at some remove on the other ridge.

The white-metal-panel belvedere houses the handicapped elevator and signals the staff entry to the complex from the arrival plaza.
Below: *The grand stairway leads from the plaza to the museum and was designed to be a gathering place.*

From the terraces of the cafeteria and restaurant one can look across to the arrival plaza and North Quad.

It is possible to read the Getty Center as a kind of ecclesiastical analogy—the museum being like a cathedral and the Research Institute approximating a monastery; the one being open to the general public and the other being reserved for scholars. At risk of carrying this too far, it is even possible to claim that the entrance plaza, paved in travertine, is akin to the traditional *parvis*, just as the museum approach may be read as the cathedral steps on which visitors may sit and look down onto the entry plaza. While there is no campanile, the museum lobby assumes the form of a cylindrical tower, its skylight functioning as a vertical feature visible as much from without as from within the museum courtyard. At the same time, this light magnifies the sense of space and highlights the stone, giving it a certain grandeur. To one side of this lobby, two small theaters, accommodating forty and sixty persons respectively, provide for general orientation and the display of introductory films, while beneath there is a 150-seat lecture hall reached by a stair.

The itinerary through the different pavilions of the museum encourages the visitor to step, from time to time, into the open air so as to experience the framed views of Bel Air and the distant, snowcapped San Gabriel Mountains. This breathtaking easterly panorama establishes a link between the architecture and its surroundings. The challenge was to bring the distant horizons into the space, not as a continuous panorama but as landscape vistas that come in and out of view.

While I am convinced that the museum galleries will be appreciated as much for their form and lighting levels as for the material they contain, recent draconian reduction in the levels of natural light, particularly in the transitional spaces between the galleries proper and the adjacent interior and external courts and terraces, can only serve, in my view, to undermine the initial concept of the museum sequence. In order to overcome "museum fatigue," brought on by both absence of natural light and insufficient spatial variation, the museum had been expressly designed to provide a series of transitional and optional outdoor spaces. This concept of a California garden museum is now on the verge of being seriously compromised by the last-minute addition of permanent light screens and black-out panels in the transitional spaces. Instead of modulating the light with adjustable screens according to the type of space,

By May 1997 the construction of the
museum was close to completion and
its courtyard and fountain were
beginning to take shape.
Opposite above: *The trellised terrace
over the entrance to the decorative-
arts galleries between museum clusters two and three.*
Opposite below: *In the museum courtyard there are specially chosen stone
benches from the quarry in Italy.*

the season of the year, and the time of day, the curatorial staff have decided to lower the levels of natural light throughout the entire museum. Aside from creating a certain monotonous lighting, the darkening of the transitional spaces will also produce an uncomfortable glare as one passes from the inside to the outside space.

In retrospect all of this seems a replay of an earlier struggle that Michael Palladino and I lost over the natural light in the auditorium, which originally had been designed with a picture window on one side. This would have had the double virtue of not only naturally lighting the auditorium during the day but also providing a framed view of the Santa Monica Mountains to the west. The window would have been fully equipped with a scrim to diffuse the rays of the evening sun and with a black-out shade to facilitate the projection of slides, video, and film during the day. The Getty was not interested and insisted on a totally blacked-out box, save for the diffused clerestory light washing the back wall of the space. We resolved this impasse with an odd compromise in which the window was installed but sealed off with Sheetrock, so that it might at some date be reopened should a future administration come to realize the virtue of such a feature.

While the exterior walls of the museum may convey the sense of a monolithic mass, the internal articulation of the pavilions presents a more fragmented, open-ended formation, bound together by the museum courtyard. The atrium walls within each pavilion cluster are dressed in a stone similar to the exterior travertine cladding. Incidental large blocks of rough-cut stone were introduced amid this dressed stone as scaling devices and as a reminder that stone needs to be wrenched from the bowels of the earth. Many of these rough-cut stones include traces of fossilized leaves and small animals, some eight to ten million years old.

I had spotted these discarded, malformed, fossilized fragments when I first visited Carlo Mariotti's travertine quarry near Rome. I asked Carlo to give us one, with the understanding that I would name it after him and insert it into the travertine wall flanking the pool in the second pavilion cluster. Thereafter I indulged in a game of incorporating similar stones into different parts of the fabric, first cryptically commemorating Carlo's family, his wife and his sons, and then certain key

On every level of the museum, from the courtyard to the elevated terraces, there are places to sit and relax in the open air after visiting the various galleries.

Overleaf: *The upper-level passageway connects the temporary-exhibition gallery to the museum entry rotunda, which serves as a focal point for the museum courtyard.*

The pedestrian causeway, which runs
from the museum to the trust office,
connects to a covered loggia that
leads to the Conservation Institute.
Opposite: The courtyard of the Conservation Institute provides a relaxing
outdoor space for the Getty staff.
Right: The top of an exterior circular
staircase

The trust office and Conservation Institute are connected by semicovered and
covered passageways. The image
(opposite) *shows the double-level link-
age between the two and the museum.*
Opposite below: *A detail of the façade
of the trust office*

The terraces, loggias, sun-breakers,
stairs, pedestrian causeways, and
gardens that define the exterior
spaces of the north and east buildings
Overleaf: *The terrace of the restaurant/
café provides magnificent views of the
Santa Monica Mountains.*

Above: *The offices and the study spaces of the Research Institute overlook the cylindrical courtyard and circular skylight over the scholars' reading space.*
Opposite: *A ramp, which encloses the courtyard with views to the garden and beyond, provides interior circulation.*
Overleaf: *View from the helipad located at the northern end of the* campus looking toward the auditorium and trust office

members of the Getty team. This was, in truth, a kind of secret Duchampian puzzle, since the stones are not inscribed and the names are only registered on the drawings. Only I and my staff know which stone is meant to honor whom. All of these stones were inserted in the dressed-stone surfaces at eye level or below, and provide a heightened awareness of the material by their subtle contrast.

The experience of moving through the museum is full of surprises. One of my favorite locations is the space between the third and fourth pavilion clusters, where a door opens onto a terrace looking over the southern promontory of the museum. This position offers one of the most spectacular panoramic views from the entire complex—a 180-degree sweep from the ocean across the city and into Bel Air. On a clear day, one can see all the way to San Diego. Out of respect for the privacy of the Brentwood residents, visitors cannot enter the cactus garden on the south promontory, the stone-clad form of which affords a topographical flourish and anchors the museum complex to the ridge. It is unfortunate that visitors cannot complete their experience of the Getty by walking to the end of this ridge, but the Brentwood Homeowners' Association thought this would infringe on their privacy. Early on in the design process when one vocal resident was invited up to the promontory, I asked her to point out her home. She was concerned that the visitors would look out over her swimming pool and see her sunbathing in the nude. After some moments of searching in vain through the heavily wooded landscape for the unmistakable profile of her own unique home and pool, she exclaimed in exasperation: "Well, I can't see it, but I know it's out there somewhere."

Even though it was known early on that white paneling would not be acceptable as a primary exterior material, I was able to include some pure white accents here and there: in the cantilevered reception canopy over the upper tram station; in the adjacent cylindrical elevator; in the museum entry rotunda; on the perimeter of the courtyard of the Research Institute; and, last but not least, in the cantilevered canopies that extend over the main entrance of every public building. Viewed in isolation, the off-white metal revetment seems appropriate, and seen

Two different interior office spaces within the Education and Conservation Institutes showing the way in which each office interior was tailor-made to suit the specific requirements of each program.
Opposite: One of the feature stones that were inserted at a few key intervals throughout the complex

Outdoor terrace and sun-screening loggia for the cafeteria of the food-services building, facing north over the Santa Monica Mountains
Below: In the auditorium, the cast-glass-and-metal screens on each side of the projection screen can be rotated to fine-tune the acoustics.

against the pure white, it obviously has an ocher tint closer to the color of the stone. In time, the sun will bleach the travertine cladding to a lighter color, but it will never become white. It will always be distinguishable from the off-white metal paneling in both color and texture. What pleases me now is that both the stone and the off-white paneling reflect the light of day in a different way, changing hour by hour and taking on an earthy hue when they catch the rays of the setting sun.

I recall standing in the North Quad late one Sunday afternoon in September 1997 and discovering that the buildings no longer needed me. It was a little like having to recognize that the children have grown up, only this time I would be the one leaving home. Every architect involved with a work to which he has given his heart knows the pangs of separation involved. Up to the point of completion the project remains in your personal charge. The drawings may have long since determined the general outcome, but you are still adjusting minor details of the work up to the last minute. You want it to be right, and details become ever more important as the work nears completion. Yet, inevitably, there comes a moment when you must hand it over and it becomes "theirs." As you leave, the building takes on a life of its own. You are no longer in control and you have to face the fact that from now on you will be judged solely by what you leave behind.

Such mixed feelings touch the very essence of one's life as an architect. It is certainly satisfying to know that one leaves behind a physical testimony to one's passage through the world. But one also feels a real sense of joy at being able to affect people's lives in a positive way. It may seem foolishly utopian to imagine that one can make the world a better place by building one kind of building rather than another. At the same time, an architect, particularly one who works in an urban setting, bears a large responsibility because, while his design may be selected by an independent jury, he nonetheless imposes his own style and taste on the occupants of his work and on those who will visit or use the building in the future.

In my Gold Medal address to the AIA in February 1997, I touched on the social responsibility of the architect, and rather pedantically dwelt on the need for the profession to address the economic and social deprivation that is most evident in our failure to provide adequate housing for all social classes. I argued that we must begin to recognize publicly those who are compelled by poverty to live in squalor and who have been stripped of fundamental human rights. True, the architect is neither a politician nor a social worker, but I still believe that in addition to playing a political role as a private citizen, an architect can further influence the livability of cities by creating appropriate civic spaces. I went on to note that all too frequently today, "new buildings are perceived as being little more than commodities, with little connection to either the community or the topography." I pointed out that a new kind of public space had come into being in the form of mega–shopping centers, bureaucratic complexes, and sports facilities of every conceivable kind. One of the challenges that architecture now faces is to give a shape to these new public spaces that conveys a sense of collective responsibility and enables them to become an integral part of the urban experience. Finally, I turned to the issue of durability and the need to create works of quality that will endure rather than allow the act of building to degenerate into one more commodity.

While still occupied with the myriad final details of construction of the Getty Center, I began to turn my attention to other projects that had been somewhat neglected until now. In fall of 1996, we had won a limited competition to build a new Church for the Year 2000 in an outlying working-class district of Rome. In February 1997 I had the honor of showing our proposal to Pope John Paul II. Elsewhere in Europe, I was working on a small Hans Arp museum on a site overlooking the Rhine at Rolandseck near Bonn and in Munich the development of a long-standing plan for a new Siemens corporate headquarters. In the United States we were overseeing construction of federal courthouses in Islip, New York, and Phoenix, Arizona.

Still I had no illusion that any of it could fill the immense void that would be left in my life with the completion of the Getty. While I braced for the praise and criticism that would inevitably follow the project's conclusion, I knew the Getty Center could stand on its own. Of course, I could not help wondering how the work would change over time. I knew that in the lush California climate the landscape and the vegetation

The mandatory fire stairs that in an inclement northern climate would be enclosed are here left open and used to provide staff members with convenient and easy access between different departments.

The terrace and the semicylindrical library of the Conservation Institute look over the San Diego Freeway and Bel Air to the east.

would modify, if not soften, the Center's profile. I was sure that visitors and staff would soon become quite familiar with the Getty and adapt its form to their needs. Indeed, this was in the process of happening already. It was clear to me that, sooner or later, the Center would acquire that aura of "banality" so prized by the great French architect Auguste Perret: namely, that the building would appear as if it had always existed. Above all, I was conscious that the success of the entire enterprise would depend on how the general public responded to it. While all cultural institutions are in some sense elitist, we certainly planned the Getty with the idea of sharing art with the world at large. If this happens, it will enrich the lives of the people of Los Angeles.

Despite this optimism, I cannot help feeling that the Getty Center will not be easily repeated. In the past it was not unusual for men like J. Paul Getty to bequeath their private collections to the public. Today this liberal tradition is being eclipsed by a global opportunism that feels little responsibility for the well-being of society as a whole. The very notion of a national cultural identity and sense of social destiny is threatened. The Getty represents a generosity of spirit that, I fear, will be increasingly hard to find in the future.

Those familiar with contemporary architecture will no doubt concur that my approach is evolutionary rather than revolutionary. While the creation of tectonic form must entail the introduction of totally new elements, my work remains grounded in the heroic tradition of the modern movement dating back to the end of the 1920s. I would rather be remembered for the overall civic balance of my work and for its modulation of light and space rather than for any kind of idiosyncratic display of form as an end in itself.

Despite the current cult of instant celebrity to which architects are no exception, architecture remains a practice that is still largely anonymous. But, like the cinema, the ultimate media artwork of our time, architecture remains a decidedly collective expression, just as infinite in terms of time and manpower as it was in the Middle Ages. There can be no sole creator in any structure that is larger than the average middle-class house, and it is this sobering fact that distinguishes architecture from any other form of fine art. To put it differently, the Getty Center would simply not exist were it not for the innumerable architects,

The Research Institute and restaurant/café have reciprocal views from the terraces to the mountains beyond.

*Garden space of the Conservation
Institute looking west between the
curved wall of the entrance lobby and
the cylindrical elevator tower*
Opposite: *The entrance canopy to the
auditorium forms a striking silhouette
against the sky.*
Overleaf: *The east elevation of the
Conservation Institute and the
museum, clad in stone, crown the
hilltop.*

The terraces, staircases, sun screens, and balconies of the Getty serve not only to connect the different buildings but also to provide visual links between the buildings and the landscape.

Throughout the complex, framed views of the surrounding landscape focus one's attention and provide extraordinary views in every direction.

engineers, technicians, artisans, and workaday builders who assisted me in this endeavor for thirteen long years. To all of them I owe an irredeemable debt of gratitude.

But none of this would have happened had it not been for the existence of the Getty as an institution. As every architect knows, good clients are as rare as, if not rarer than, good architects. Thus the way in which the Getty Center has come into being is due as much to Harold Williams, Stephen Rountree, and John Walsh as it is, say, to Michael Palladino and me, not to mention the ever watchful eyes of all the innumerable others who in one way or another have contributed to its form: from the trustees to the construction workers who have worked for countless hours across the surface of the site. By now we can all claim that we have helped to build the Getty, and this, in the last analysis, is surely enough.

Permissions Acknowledgments and
Photographic Credits

Grateful acknowledgment is made to the
following for permission to reprint previously published material:

Casabella: Excerpt from editorial commentary on Richard Meier and the Getty Center
of Los Angeles by Francesco Dal Co
(*Casabella,* February 1997). Reprinted by
permission of *Casabella.*

The Harvard Architecture Review: Excerpt
from interview with Nancy Englander on
the Getty Museum (*The Harvard Architecture Review,* Fall 1985, No. 6). Reprinted by
permission of *The Harvard Architecture
Review.*

Time Inc.: Excerpt from "Grand New Getty"
by Kurt Andersen (*Time* magazine, Oct. 21,
1991), copyright © 1991 by Time Inc.
Reprinted by permission of Time Inc.

All photographs by Richard Meier except as
follows: pages 66–7 © Timothy Hursley;
pages 84–5 © Tom Bonner; page 89 © Grant
Mudford; pages 112–13 © Jock Pottle/Esto

About the Author

Richard Meier is one of the preeminent architects of the twentieth century. Among his award-winning buildings are the High Museum of Atlanta, the Canal+ television headquarters in Paris, and the acclaimed Museum of Contemporary Art in Barcelona. He has received the highest honors in the field, including the 1997 Gold Medal from the American Institute of Architects, the Praemium Imperiale, and the Pritzker Architecture Prize.

About the Type

The text of this book was set in
WTC Our Bodoni, designed by
Massimo Vignelli and Tom Carnese
in 1989. It is based on Giambattista
Bodoni's design from 1798.

Composed by North Market Street
Graphics, Lancaster, Pennsylvania

Printed and bound by Quebecor,
The Book Press, Brattleboro, Vermont

Based on a design by Massimo Vignelli